Disabling Characters

Disability Studies in Education

Susan L. Gabel and Scot Danforth
General Editors

Vol. 18

The Disability Studies in Education series is part of
the Peter Lang Education list.
Every volume is peer reviewed and meets
the highest quality standards for content and production.

PETER LANG
New York • Bern • Frankfurt • Berlin
Brussels • Vienna • Oxford • Warsaw

PATRICIA A. DUNN

Disabling Characters

REPRESENTATIONS OF DISABILITY IN YOUNG ADULT LITERATURE

PETER LANG
New York • Bern • Frankfurt • Berlin
Brussels • Vienna • Oxford • Warsaw

Library of Congress Cataloging-in-Publication Data
Dunn, Patricia A.
Disabling characters: representations of disability in young adult literature /
Patricia A. Dunn.
pages cm. — (Disability studies in education; Vol. 18)
Includes bibliographical references and index.
1. People with disabilities in literature. 2. Characters and characteristics in literature.
3. Young adult literature—History and criticism. I. Title.
PN56.5.H35D86   809'.933561—dc23   2014048950
ISBN 978-1-4331-2623-9 (hardcover)
ISBN 978-1-4331-2622-2 (paperback)
ISBN 978-1-4539-1508-0 (e-book)
ISSN 1548-7210

Bibliographic information published by **Die Deutsche Nationalbibliothek**.
Die Deutsche Nationalbibliothek lists this publication in the "Deutsche
Nationalbibliografie"; detailed bibliographic data are available
on the Internet at http://dnb.d-nb.de/.

The paper in this book meets the guidelines for permanence and durability
of the Committee on Production Guidelines for Book Longevity
of the Council of Library Resources.

To Ken

TABLE OF CONTENTS

INTRODUCTION

Why write a book examining representations of disability in young adult (YA) literature? To answer that question, I start with the premise that the status quo is not acceptable. All sorts of barriers prevent people from living their lives to the fullest, including how forces in society make them feel about themselves. Many of these forces are hidden from the very people (including myself) who participate, perhaps obliviously, in maintaining these forces: harmful assumptions about race, class, gender, age, income level, sexual orientation, ethnicity, and disability. While assumptions about all these groups should be named and challenged, the last one listed—disability—is perhaps the one least likely to be examined from a critical perspective, at least regarding YA literature. Many barriers contributing to disability are material or attitudinal; either way, they are built. They are constructed. And whatever is constructed can be named, mitigated, or removed.

Fiction can affect the way real people are treated. It can open readers' minds to entrenched discriminatory attitudes, or it can be complicit with those attitudes, making them worse. The "disabling characters" in the title of this book has a double meaning. It refers to two types of characters who have the power to affect beliefs: one for good and one for ill:

1) Some characters are "disabling" in a good way because they challenge or "disable" myths about disability, and what happens to those characters can help draw attention to constructed barriers to real people with disabilities. Fictional characters can provide direct verbal challenges to myths and stereotypes expressed by other characters. Or, characters with impairments might display a refreshing agency in the plot structure: they make decisions and act in ways that determine their own fate, thus countering pervasive narratives that depict them as pitiable, helpless, sad, etc.

2) Some characters are "disabling" in a bad way: they can make discrimination and exclusion worse for real people with disabilities. This "disabling" may happen in several ways: the stereotypical way in which disabled characters are portrayed; a tired plot structure in which they die or get cured at the end, suggesting there's no place for disability in mainstream society; and unchallenged discriminatory remarks reflecting assumptions of an ableist society, that is, a society that privileges so called "able-bodied" people.

I believe that reading high-quality disability-themed fiction can begin to break down the us/them dichotomy so harmful in our society and reduce barriers to full accessibility. Lest this belief sound too naïve, let me hasten to add that there are many potential hazards in reading fiction about disability. If characters with disabilities are depicted as pitiable victims, or as those who must be rescued by others, or as unlikely heroes who save the day, the novel can simply perpetuate harmful views of disability and cast people with disabilities as "other." However, reading nuanced novels with disabled main characters, followed by responsible discussions, can get students thinking critically about disability.

Discussions are critical. Done poorly, discussions, too, can reinscribe stereotypes. However, well-placed critical questions about what the text is doing can help readers identify harmful views and to comment on their appropriateness in a just world. Even a text that displays unchallenged stereotypes about disability can be recruited to question those stereotypes if teachers pose critical questions. Sadly, as we will see, such higher-level questions are rare in public materials available on the web where topics for class discussion are typically limited to plot structure, theme, and literary elements.

I argue that as we are selecting the novels and stories we use in class and the activities we design to accompany them, we should instead consider questions such as these:

- Do some stories about disability make societal conditions better or worse for those concerned with disability rights?
- What effects might different stories have on readers with a variety of life experiences?
- How might story endings affect readers' views of disability?
- To what extent do published reception documents (discussion questions, study guides, and quizzes) for those books challenge or perpetuate harmful stereotypes?
- How might analysis of disability-related YA novels and their reception documents break down constructed barriers to full participation?

I intend these and other questions listed throughout this book to be adapted and modified by imaginative teachers for use with a variety of texts, and to act as a counterweight to more conventional questions about vocabulary, plot, and symbols.

Researchers do report some positive change in the ways characters with disabilities are depicted in novels. In her overview of research, Eve Tal reports that portrayals are gradually becoming more realistic, in contrast to common portrayals in the nineteenth century in which characters with disabilities "were inevitably passive, ever cheerful, long-suffering, and dead by the close of the book" (1). It would seem that depictions of people with disability had nowhere to go but up. As Biklen, Bogdan, and Blatt point out in their essay in a 1977 book on TV programming for children, "The mass media has linked ugliness and disabilities with evil and violence for a long time" (3).[1] They continue, "Disability labels often act as cues for images of dependence, pity, guilt, childishness, incompetence, unusual personality formation, sexless, and sexual deviance." What they say about television could also be applied to young adult novels: "Television can either perpetuate these stereotypes or promote more positive images of people who have disabilities" (3). In a very early articulation of what will later become known as "the social model" of disability, they write that "the primary cause of their [people with disabilities] dependence may not be the disability so much as society's unwillingness to accommodate for disabilities" (5). This examination of how society contributes to the effects of impairment is what has been hard to find in YA literature, at least until recently.

The Purpose of This Book

Using a theoretical lens influenced by disability studies, an approach that examines society's role in exacerbating whatever impairments individuals may have, I will juxtapose selected YA novels about disability and discuss the effects they seem to have. I will also analyze selected published reception documents on these works: summaries, reviews, discussion questions, reading guides, and quizzes that shape readers' understandings of these fictional pieces. Using literary and rhetorical analysis, my goal is to make visible the underlying assumptions about disability present, but not always immediately evident, in these texts and in materials about them.

Young adult (YA) novels today provide one of the few growth areas for print publications, and the last ten years have seen an uptick in high-quality YA novels centering on disability. Because they have adolescent protagonists, take up contemporary problems, and are generally written in a style that appeals to young people, YA novels are among the works most likely to be actually read by adolescents and discussed in their classes. These discussions, however well intentioned, have the potential to reinforce harmful stereotypes about disability. In contrast, discussions informed by a disability studies or disability rights perspective—one that draws attention to the constructedness of disability—can help readers develop more informed, enlightened views of disability and make society more accessible for all people. Because so many novels do not focus on disability or even mention it as a part of life for so many people, it's critical that the few texts that *are* read, and the rare discussions about disability that *do* take place, do more than support the status quo regarding society's still very limiting view of disability. Some texts should invite readers to question the status quo. This questioning of cultural ideologies and their effect on disabling conditions appears only rarely in YA novels, and almost never in reception documents used in the schools to discuss these texts.[2]

My purpose in writing this book is to promote ways of talking about disability that will invite the public—especially English Language Arts teachers and students in middle and high schools—to develop informed, critical perspectives on how disability is represented in our society and what role society plays in the construction of disability. In my analysis, I treat books more as cultural artifacts than as works of art, though I do make value judgments based on a variety of criteria, some originating in the conventional western literary tradition, some from other value systems.

Disability Studies in the Schools

The Society for Disability Studies is an expanding, interdisciplinary non-profit organization primarily centered in higher education. It states in its mission that it "seeks to augment understanding of disability in all cultures and historical periods, to promote greater awareness of the experiences of disabled people, and to advocate for social change." (SDS website). The number of graduate programs in disability studies is growing, and there are many college courses influenced by this international movement. The K-12 schools, however, have so far been much less affected.

In the Introduction to her book, *Disability Studies in Education*, Susan Lynn Gabel points to the slow pace at which disability studies has influenced education in the schools:

> In spite of the growing influence of disability studies over the last three decades, educational researchers, by and large, have come late to the movement that began officially with the proclamation by the Union of Physically Impaired Against Segregation (UPIAS) in 1972 in the United Kingdom and with the founding of the Society for Disability Studies (SDS) in the United States in 1982 (1).

Much work still needs to be done in order to incorporate ideas from disability studies into concrete but theorized practice that teachers in the schools can use. Later in the same Introduction, Gabel points to the importance of asking pointed questions about actual practice:

> How can education be organized to prevent institutionalized oppression of any student? This question assumes that without educational praxis, disablement (or other forms of oppression) will occur. These questions are not asked often by scholars in disability studies, but they are questions that disability studies in education must ask and answer. (10)

Acknowledging the wide-ranging nature of the phrase, "disability studies in education," Gabel writes, "One could define disability studies in education as the use and application of disability studies assumptions and methods to educational issues and problems" (10).

Other scholars also highlight the need to update professionals in the schools to the game-changing theoretical perspective offered by disability studies: society's role in disabling individuals. As Robin M. Smith and Nirmala Erevelles point out, discussions of this view of disability are rare in conventional education environments. In their review of two books, one by Paul Longmore and one by Rod Michalko, they critique the status quo:

> Many of our own students in teacher education and educational administration are usually accustomed to discussions of disability that are focused more on "what is wrong" with their disabled students and on the pedagogical and administrative strategies for "fixing" these students. Conspicuously silent in their courses is any discussion about the political nature of disability...." (32)

They use an apt quotation from Longmore to describe the social model of disability, in which the "disability" is "not somatic but social: prejudice and discrimination, inaccessibility, and the lack of accommodations" (Longmore, 2003, p. 2; qtd in Smith and Erevelles, 33). Our schools need to explore further this perspective on what is really "disabling" in our culture.

Because fiction is still a significant part of the middle and high school English Language Arts curriculum, text selection and question design can help young readers become more aware of the "prejudice and discrimination, inaccessibility and the lack of accommodations" Longmore describes. Although disability studies has done much to call harmful assumptions into question, school-aged adolescents have not yet sufficiently benefitted from research, scholarship, and discussions that are still mostly taking place in the academic circles of higher education. It's important, therefore, to choose novels carefully, and to design discussion questions that help students think critically about the implications about what the novel says, or implies, about disability.

What Literary Texts Can Do

Books with an obvious intention to instruct or teach are frowned upon in western society. If a work is called "didactic," it is being called preachy, boring, and of poor quality. In the 19th century, books for children were commonly written for instructive or moral purposes. Today, those purposes are frequently listed in writing advice columns as one of the first qualities in YA novels to be avoided. Contemporary YA novels, which emerged in the middle of the last century, may well have a lesson or message embedded in them, but the most successful ones make something else the focus of the plot: the love story, the mystery, the culminating game or show, etc. But to get whatever lesson—if there is one—in a text, readers first have to read it. And some novels that seem to have lesson-giving as a goal may not be well-crafted enough for readers to finish.

In western culture, overtly didactic novels are often contrasted, with disdain, to ones that seem to have what many consider to be a higher, mimetic, literary, "universal," or artistic purpose: the "Art for art's sake" view. (See Edgar Allan Poe's "The Poetic Principle.") The supposed "universal" quality of "good literature" has been questioned by many, not least of whom is Sherman Alexie, who, in a profile about him in *The Writer*, critiques this idea: "When 'universal' is used as an adjective of praise in the mainstream media, it means nothing more than writing about the lives of minorities in a way that can be understood by white people, he says" (McNally 28). Writers featuring characters with disabilities who wish their story to have "universal" appeal must also grapple with decisions about what non-disabled readers will understand.

In the introduction to their 1984 book-length annotated bibliography, Baskin and Harris point out that many books "do not succeed as literature" (32). They say that books "are not effective pulpits and the use of literature to instigate social transformations has had limited success" (33). Here is the last sentence in their long introduction, however: "Books are among the most potent tools available for promoting attitudinal change" (49). So the trick for such books seems to be to educate or influence readers, and to change attitudes for the better, but to do it through a kind of subterfuge. Once the purpose to improve society becomes too clear, once readers see the strings on the marionettes, the book is no longer eligible for the "literature" shelf, at least in Western literary circles.

Similarly, Hazlett, Sweeney, and Reins write that "An educator's primary task is teaching novels well, rather than using them to change student views…" (209). Their article, however, is entitled, "Using Young Adult Literature Featuring LGBTQ Adolescents With Intellectual and/or Physical Disabilities to Strengthen Classroom Inclusion." So their basically good advice about selecting quality texts is also framed by this somewhat conflicting judgment. So deeply ingrained is the learned distaste for novels that "teach," that even those scholars whose main purpose seems to be to promote the use of novels on LGBTQ to change attitudes or promote inclusion feel the need to first go on record as disapproving of novels with a lesson.

Of course, many "literary" texts also teach us something about the world, though they do it subtly and artistically. Few would argue that *To Kill A Mockingbird* is a literary novel, but its "Don't be a racist" message is also strong. Shakespeare's plays, arguably some of the most artistic texts ever written, also teach us something about how to live or how not to live. *Romeo and Juliet* teaches us about how not to destroy our young people through senseless, generational disputes. *Macbeth* shows what too much ambition, greed, and cruelty can do. *Othello* shows us the results of jealousy and of acting too fast; Hamlet shows what acting too slowly can do.[3] Those interpretations are reductive and subject to debate, of course. But the point is that a text can be both literary and instructive.

I, too, dislike preachy, lesson-giving texts. However, no text can escape its implications. Post-structuralist theory recognizes that a text cannot help but reinforce or challenge existing assumptions in society. In distinguishing between the older type of adolescent novel and contemporary ones, Roberta Seelinger Trites associates the former with "our romantic belief in growth" and the latter with "our postmodern awareness of the socially constructed limitations of power..." (*Disturbing the Universe*, 20). She sees the modern YA novel as a genre that "very self-consciously problematizes the relationship of the individual to the institutions that construct his or her subjectivity" (20).

Other scholars have addressed what may be seen in the West as unconventional value systems and their attendant criteria for "good literature." Chinua Achebe explains one such contrasting value system, for example, in an interview with Charles H. Rowell in *Callaloo*. Achebe contrasts the purpose of art and literature in western cultures with a different purpose in Nigeria, where "... art is in the service of the community. There is no apology at all about that. Art is invented to make the life of the community easier, not to make it more difficult" (Rowell 86). Responding to Western criticism of African literature that it is "so political," (87), Achebe emphasizes that readers in his culture "are expecting literature to say something important to help them in their struggle with life" (Rowell 88).

In the 1980s, feminist literary critic Jane Tompkins challenged the "enduring themes" approach to literature and called for "a redefinition of literature and literary study" in a way that had more respect for texts that do "cultural work" (200):

> I see their plots and characters as providing society with a means of thinking about itself, defining certain aspects of a social reality which the authors and their readers shared, dramatizing its conflicts, and recommending solutions. It is the notion of literary texts as doing work, expressing and shaping the social context that produced them... ." (200).

Like the writing Achebe describes, the novels Tompkins values are "attempts to redefine the social order" (Tompkins xi).

In Judith Fetterley's groundbreaking text, *The Resisting Reader*, she argues, as did Adrienne Rich, for the need to "re-read" (viii). Re-reading is necessary because "…what we read affects us—drenches us, to use Rich's language, in its assumptions, and that to avoid drowning in this drench of assumptions we must learn to re-read" (viii). Although Fetterley's resistance was to misogynist assumptions in "classic" American fiction, her concept of "the resisting reader" is useful here in discussing disabling or ableist texts, which often blithely and uncritically draw upon disability myths or stereotypes, thus cementing them further. Such texts will no doubt continue to be taught in the schools, but teachers and students can learn to resist them in ways Fetterley describes.

My analysis in this book has been influenced by the culture in which I was first exposed to literary texts and by the literary, rhetorical, and cultural theories I've encountered over the years. All this has persuaded me that every literary text does cultural work, for good or for ill, regardless of its perceived quality or its author's intention, which, as the New Critics taught, could not or should not be determined. (This was the "intentional fallacy" they warned against.)

Because texts are so powerful—well-written or not, YA or not, "classic" or not—responsible educators need to do more than conduct discussions of themes and literary elements. Part of being a critical or even, dare I say, a "close reader" of the kind the Common Core claims to promote, is to be alert to what a text seems to imply, to analyze a text's "cultural work" (Tompkins), and to become "a resisting reader" (Fetterley) if that cultural work perpetuates harmful stereotypes. In this book, I want to help teachers and their students recognize and resist discriminatory views.

Here are samples of the kinds of questions I pose in this book, some larger ones dealing with the role literary texts play in the schools, some specific to a particular text:

- Why do we read literary texts in school?
- What is privileged in the texts we choose?
- Who gains and who loses by the representations that appear in these texts?
- How is disability represented in this text?

- How is disability represented in the reception documents about that text—the online summaries, discussion questions, study guides, and quizzes?
- What are some implications of those representations for individuals in the real world?
- What "cultural work" (Jane Tompkins' phrase) does this text do? In other words, to what extent are harmful stereotypes about disability cultivated, disrupted, or both?
- How might hidden, harmful assumptions about disability be recognized so that students might become "resisting readers" (Fetterley)?
- If this text cultivates harmful assumptions about disability, but the text is going to be read anyway, what questions can be posed about this book to get readers to re-think those assumptions? What companion text could be read in order to contrast the representations of disability in one with the other?

Imaginative teachers will come up with their own questions, or modify these or other questions to best fit their own objectives, curricular needs, and reading selections. These questions need not replace the typical questions posed about texts, but may be incorporated into questions about inference, an important skill for readers at any level to develop.

Terminology and Disability Status

I am uncomfortable using some terms in this book. In our language, the words "abled" and "disabled" are already infused with harmful us/them binaries and assumptions that are difficult to avoid when writing about this topic. This automatic dividing of people into groups sets up one group as "normal," as authoritative, as having power. It can set the other group up as not "normal," or as identified primarily through their "disability." Such binarizing also renders invisible the fact that everyone has, had, or will have in his or her lifetime, what might be called a disability or an impairment.[4] This binary and these terms also hide the role we all play in contributing to conditions which create or intensify disability, such as not working to eliminate physical barriers like stairs and narrow doorways, or intellectual barriers such as print-only textbooks.

The words "abled" and "disabled" are not the only terms that needed sorting out. I considered whether to use the phrase "people with disabilities" or

"disabled people." I first heard the phrase "people with disabilities," often ab-
breviated to "PWD," over twenty years ago at a Conference on College Composition and Communication. It was used and recommended by colleagues
in CCCC's disability community, and I agree with the reasoning behind it:
that it stresses people first, not their disability. However, in summarizing Rod
Michalko's critique of "people-first" language, Smith and Erevelles write that
'People-with...' generalizes disability as a condition and thus precludes the
possibility of disability as an identity" (35). In addition, some see "impairment" as referring to a limitation an individual might have, while "disability"
refers to limits or barriers society constructs which disable people with impairments. In her own discussion of terminology in *Claiming Disability*, Simi
Linton points out:

> Beginning in the early 90s *disabled people* has been increasingly used in disability
> studies and disability rights circles when referring to the constituency group. Rather
> than maintaining disability as a secondary characteristic, *disabled* has become a mark-
> er of the identity that the individual and group wish to highlight and call attention
> to. (13)

Linton also explains, "The use of *nondisabled* is strategic: to center disability"
(13). We do not yet live in a society in which complete avoidance of either
phrase—"people with disabilities" or "disabled people"—is possible. So in this
text I use them interchangeably, acknowledging here that they have different
effects and are both problematic.

In her essay in *Disability and the Teaching of Writing*, Deb Martin points
out the subtle but powerful role that an author's status plays in a text, and she
suggests that the author's status be made known:

> Considering that it is the textbook author/editor who is selecting the material, posing
> the questions about the material, and determining how students will write about the
> issues, perhaps the subjective editorial stance should be made known to the readers.
> No matter what that status is, readers, following cultural linguistic codes, interpret
> that the authors are situated in the dominant, that is, able-bodied, position. (83).

In the interest of this disclosure, let me say that as of this writing, I consider
myself a non-disabled ally of people with disabilities. Like most people in
this culture, I've been influenced by ableist assumptions throughout my life,
and, in spite of my best intentions, I'm sure they continue to influence me
in subtle and invisible ways. For the last thirty years I've been reading about
disability and attending and participating in conference sessions on disability,

researching it, writing about it, and trying to enact a more inclusive pedagogy. I've learned much from my generous colleagues at the Conference on College Composition and Communication (Brenda Jo Brueggemann, Jay Dolmage, Stephanie Kerschbaum, Cynthia Lewiecki-Wilson, Margaret Price, Amy Vidali, and many more), and everyone I've served with on the CCCC Committee on Disability Issues. I have been influenced greatly by their leadership, insight, and knowledge of the field.

I cannot draw upon my own experience living with a disability in this culture, though I have a close relative who does have that experience, and I have seen the endless barriers he has had to contend with both as a child and as an adult. My mother, too, when she used a wheelchair on and off late in her life, faced barriers: stairs, narrow doorways, inaccessible private and public buildings, and people addressing their comments to me, not to her. On a personal level, accessibility is important to me because although I am a TAB (temporarily able-bodied), I may need a more accessible environment for myself one day, and because people I know, as well as millions of people I don't know, need that accessibility now.

On a professional level, accessibility is important to me because I wish to make my own classes, and those of my colleagues, more accessible to all students. And I want the future teachers I work with to be more informed about accessibility issues in their own classes and institutions. I am aware of James Charlton's "nothing about us without us" stance regarding disability, which I respect. I do not presume to speak for people with disabilities, nor am I able to do so. My judgments in this book are about characters in novels and short stories. In this book, I discuss characters with disabilities in young adult literature, and I use them as a vehicle to weave in what I've learned about disabilities, literature, rhetoric, reading, and teaching. My hope is that issues raised here can help others frame their discussions of similar novels so that readers can begin to imagine—and help build—a different world view.

The Chapters

Chapter 1: Agency, Rebellion, and Challenging the Status Quo

Juxtaposed in this chapter are two books about a summer camp for people with disabilities: *Accidents of Nature* (Henry Holt and Company, 2006), a YA novel by Harriet McBryde Johnson, a disability rights activist who used a wheelchair, and the short, often-assigned book, *The Acorn People* (Random

House, 1976), by Ron Jones, who based it on his experiences as a counselor at such a camp in the 1970s. By contrasting the different perspectives of each of the first-person narrators (Jean, who is attending this camp for the first time, and Ron, who is experiencing his first summer as a counselor), readers can learn much about harmful, but rarely questioned assumptions in our society. While both books critique the status quo regarding disability and access, one does so to a much greater degree than does the other, which may have to do with the eras in which they were written, as well as the personal experiences of their respective authors. Examining the two books as a pair reveals much about power, rebellion, and agency. I also analyze published questions and activities on the popular book by Jones.

Chapter 2: Respect, Etiquette, and the Drama of Rude Behavior

In this chapter, I discuss two recent YA novels in which the first person narrator is a high school student who is deaf: *The Dark Days of Hamburger Halpin*, by Josh Berk (Alfred A. Knopf, 2010) and *Five Flavors of Dumb*, by Antony John (Penguin, 2010). I also discuss *The Cardturner* (Delacorte, 2010), by Louis Sachar, in which the protagonist and first person narrator is a seventeen-year-old named Alton Richards, who becomes deeply involved in the life of his uncle Lester Trapp, a life-long bridge player who has recently become blind because of diabetes. Through dramatic confrontations between characters, all three of these novels provide spoken or unspoken critiques of how non-disabled people interact with those who have impairments Although lessons on respect may not be the purported "theme" or main "purpose" of these and other YA novels, selected scenes can provide a dramatic "how to" for readers who may not have had an opportunity to think about these issues. More importantly, the cultural/critical analysis provided in this chapter can bring a disability studies interpretive lens to a readership not previously exposed to it.

Chapter 3: Awakening Stories: "The Scarlet Ibis" and *The Cay*

In this chapter, I examine two popular stories that may sometimes challenge, sometimes reinforce, harmful binaries regarding disability. Paying particular attention to the endings of these texts and the conclusions they seem to invite readers to draw, this chapter will examine the frequently anthologized short story, "The Scarlet Ibis," by James Hurst, and the canonical novel, *The Cay*, by Theodore Taylor, as well as selected publically available supplemental materials used to discuss them.

Chapter 4: Carving Out an Identity

Many YA novels are about finding one's identity. But the young protagonists with disabilities in these novels often must also learn to challenge their own, internalized, socially constructed assumptions about who they are in relation to a world that has already categorized them. This chapter will examine the first-person narrators from this perspective in three YA novels, as well as some supporting materials: *Peeling the Onion*, by Wendy Orr; *The Absolutely True Diary of a Part-Time Indian*, by Sherman Alexie; and *Stoner and Spaz*, by Ron Koertge. Two of these authors (Orr and Alexie) have disabilities very similar to those of their respective protagonists, a fact that may have important implications for how disability is represented in those texts.

Chapter 5: "Normal" Talents, Rudolph Stories, and "Supercrips"

Many novels have a protagonist whose impairment plays a role in solving a crime. Such novels can reveal to oblivious readers the contributions people with disabilities can make to society, using talents or insights they have developed, sometimes because of their specific impairment. But there is a danger of these stories becoming tales of stereotypical "supercrips," who develop an almost super-human ability, whereupon they are finally accepted by their peers. I call these "Rudolph the Red-Nosed Reindeer" stories because, in the end, the individual who was formerly mocked or ignored becomes a hero who saves the day.

The message here, if not identified and challenged, is that a "successful" disabled person can't just simply be, can't just live a normal, satisfactory life without being expected either to "overcome" an impairment or to use it somehow to save the world. I will examine four YA mystery novels, some of which are able to successfully negotiate the fine line between a protagonist with unusual but "normal" talents, and a "supercrip" hero: *The London Eye Mystery*, by Siobhan Dowd; *Marcelo in the Real World* by Francisco X. Stork (both books have a protagonist on the autism spectrum); *From Charlie's Point of View*, by Richard Scrimger, in which the sleuth is blind; and *The Dark Days of Hamburger Halpin*, by Josh Berk, in which the mystery solver is deaf (a

different aspect of *Dark Days* is covered in another chapter.)[5] I will also analyze selected questions/activities related to these novels.

Some Caveats

Theoretical Approaches

I take a somewhat eclectic approach to theoretical frames. I am less concerned with the "unity" or beauty of the text itself and more interested in the
text's upending of, or blithe reliance upon, harmful assumptions in society. I
wonder if readers are absorbing or challenging the text's obvious or not-so-
obvious messages. While my primary lens is heavily influenced by scholarship
in disability studies, that lens intersects simultaneously with early feminist
theory, especially Judith Fetterley's concept of "the resisting reader" and Jane
Tompkins concept of "cultural work." Like almost everyone who has studied
literature in school, I am also heavily influenced by New Critics and their
emphasis on the structure of a text. While the New Critics made a deliberate
turn against biographical interpretations and authorial intent, I do consider
author background in my discussions. Given James Charlton's main point in
his book, *Nothing About Us Without Us*, an author's experience with disability
is highly relevant.

Spoilers

Because this book is an analysis, spoilers unavoidably appear. Readers currently reading one of the novels under discussion may wish to finish that novel
first. Alternately, even readers who have no intention of ever reading these
novels could read *Disabling Characters* for its analytical frame and discussions
of disabling assumptions also present in other literature.

Samplings

This book analyzes a sampling of YA texts that focus on disability and a sampling of reception documents about those texts. Some of the novels I discuss
in this book do an admirable job confronting and disabling harmful societal
myths regarding disability. Others try but fall short. Most do a bit of both,
which is no doubt true for many texts, both old and new. I've picked works
that I thought it would be productive to talk about together and to juxtapose,

to see what could be discovered and what issues would arise. While some of these books would be good to use as pairs, or in combination with others, sometimes the issues/problems raised in these chapters might be a good jumping off point for books not included here or not yet written. Readers are encouraged to find more such novels, as well as their supporting materials, and determine to what extent those texts work to disable harmful society assumptions or to contribute to disabling myths about disability. I intend this book as a point of departure to help readers do that.

Judgments

My judgments about these texts are meant to open conversations about all texts used in the schools and how those texts are discussed. Other readers might well have different interpretations of the fiction and reception documents analyzed in this book, as I might, too, if I were reading them in a different time and context. I hope that my sometimes pointed critiques of characters—whether these characters are "disabling" in a positive or negative way—will get students and teachers talking about representations of disability, not only in YA novels, but in other cultural artifacts.

Notes

1. I discovered this Biklen et al. reference in the Works Cited of Sharon E. Andrews' article in the *Journal of Adolescent & Adult Literacy*.
2. A number of scholars have advocated for critical discussions about fiction and disability. Sharon E. Andrews summarizes many studies that indicate that "the use of literature about disabilities can be effective in promoting awareness, understanding, and acceptance of those with disabilities and can assist in creating positive attitudes toward disabilities" 420). Emily Wopperer, too, advocates for these texts: "Children's and young adult books that portray characters with disabilities are important tools for helping all readers learn about, understand, and relate to people with disabilities" (26). In her summary of reasons to read these works, Judith Landrum goes beyond this limited purpose, adding that these works can give "disabled people characters they can identify with ...." (285). Wopperer also says these texts can help "children and young adults with disabilities to see themselves differently, more positively" (28). This latter purpose is sometimes called "bibliotherapy" (Prater 47). In their article in the *Australian Journal of Human Rights*, Helen Meekosha and Russell Shuttleworth use the phrase "critical disability studies (CDS)," which they say "is emerging as the preferred nomenclature of many scholars..." (2009). Influenced by Freire's concept of "critical consciousness," Jen Scott Curwood uses the phrase "critical pedagogy"

to describe an approach that "provides a space to question, analyze, and transform cultural ideologies and social practices" (16).

3. The contrast between Othello acting too fast and Hamlet acting too slowly I owe to a wonderful British literature scholar and professor who taught me at The University at Albany, Dr. Hugh N. Maclean.

4. In the U.K., using the social model, some have drawn a distinction between "impairment" and "disability." An "impairment" is seen as a particular limitation an individual might have, while a "disability" is the limitations and barriers constructed by society. I think that is a useful distinction, though I use those terms mostly interchangedly in this book.

5. Many thanks to Mark Letcher, whose "Off the Shelves" *English Journal* column on disability and YA literature (November 2010) informed me about *The London Eye Mystery*, *Marcelo in the Real World*, and others.

AGENCY, REBELLION, AND CHALLENGING THE STATUS QUO: *ACCIDENTS OF NATURE* AND *THE ACORN PEOPLE*

One of the main features of a disability rights perspective is that it turns the spotlight of critique on society. Instead of focusing on an individual person's ability to "overcome" an impairment and "fit" into "normal" society, scholars and activists focus on constructed societal barriers that exclude, either deliberately or obliviously, people with disabilities. While many YA novels have sections that critique mainstream society or the occasional rude behavior of several people in that society, Harriet McBryde Johnson's *Accidents of Nature*, from start to finish, calls into question society's views of disability. It is fierce in its challenge to the status quo, and the disabled characters' rebellion against mainstream society is uncompromising. This novel also handles agency in an unusual way. The disabled characters in many adult and YA novels are acted upon, rather than agents of their own lives. Often it is non-disabled characters who speak up for them, communicate for them, or discover something about themselves because of their interaction with these characters. However, *Accidents of Nature* foregrounds the characters with disabilities as the clear agents of their own lives and as agents of change. The "norms," as the non-disabled characters are called, are clearly the secondary characters and are acted upon. This novel has a refreshing in-your-face stance against the status quo, a stance that is rare, intense, and triumphant.

Accidents of Nature

The narrator is Jean, a seventeen-year-old woman who has cerebral palsy and uses a wheelchair. She sometimes cannot control her body movements, and she occasionally stutters. Set in 1970, the novel has autobiographical elements from the life of its author, Harriet McBryde Johnson, a disability rights activist and attorney who died in 2008.[1] This is Jean's first summer at "Camp Courage," run by "Norms" and designed around an ableist "Just try harder" and "Everyone's a winner" philosophy, which frustrates and angers many campers. These attitudes were still pillars of mainstream belief in 2006, when the novel was published. Jean begins the summer thinking of herself as "normal." Exposed to fellow camper Sara, a rebel who reads Marx and also Erving Goffman's *Stigma* (112), Jean has several identity crises throughout her ten days at camp. Her stay there is a roller coaster of emotions, and she leaves there changed forever.

Through Jean's perspective, the first-person narration invites disabled and non-disabled readers alike to identify with Jean as she comes to see the ignorance and cruelty of the "normal" world. Sometimes well intentioned, sometimes not, the camp organizers and counselors disrespect, humiliate, and sometimes abuse the campers. Through Sara's instruction and example, Jean comes to see her own limitations and her unimagined possibilities. It's an identity story for Jean, and also possibly for many readers.

Accidents of Nature is a call to action, an outrageous (in a good way) masterpiece that "teaches a lesson" in the same way *To Kill A Mockingbird* does—beautifully and artistically. This novel names, critiques, and explodes several myths about disability: that "just trying harder" will "fix" anything, that people with disabilities are sexless beings, and that walking is the ultimate goal no matter what. *Accidents of Nature* turns hegemony on its head by depicting the "norms" as outsiders, as the ones who don't get it.

But because this book is so unusual, or perhaps because I had never before read anything like it, on a first reading I felt myself skimming it in parts. I was intrigued by Jean, but I had trouble identifying with her. I became impatient with the detailed, sometimes graphic descriptions of Jean's disabled cabin mates, some of whom Jean, early in the novel, finds unpleasant to look at or listen to. I could understand the bitterness of the influential character Sara, who also uses a wheelchair and who keeps trying to change insulting activities or oppressive attitudes at the camp. Like Jean, the first-person narrator, however, I was a bit shocked and irritated by Sara's sarcasm and irony and by what

I first thought was her cruelty in calling her fellow campers "crips," or "MRs" (mentally retarded), or "spazzos."

But of all the YA novels I read for this project, this literary, mature, and challenging book is the one that affected me the most, that most changed my worldview. When I read it again, I saw every scene differently. I saw so much more in the poetic, symbolic description in the Prologue and the artistic references throughout the book to the metaphors in the first pages. I felt more of Sara's frustration with the way the camp was run and with the ableist assumptions the management made about the campers. I identified more with Jean's emotions, her embarrassment in front of a boy she has a crush on, her excitement in participating in a rebellion Sara organizes, her sadness in growing away from her family, her confidence in imagining her future.

Accidents of Nature is a coming of age story, not unusual for a YA novel. What is less usual is that this is a coming of age story about a young woman with cerebral palsy who uses a wheelchair. It is a Bildungsroman, which, as Roberta Seelinger Trites defines the term, is a novel "in which the protagonist comes of age as an adult" (10). Like most YA narrators, Jean discovers something about her identity, and she does change and mature into an adult. But before she finds that identity, there are many points along the way that shock Jean, delight her, disgust her, enrage her, and liberate her.

What is unique about this novel, however, is this: the maturing narrator also comes to see the *world* as a place that needs to change, especially in its treatment of people with disabilities. This novel is a powerful counter-narrative, a critique of society in the same way the campers' "reverse telethon" is a counter-narrative to and critique of the real life Jerry Lewis telethons that Harriet McBryde Johnson protested for fifteen years.

Young adult novels about protagonists with disabilities are becoming fairly common. The authors of many such novels are people who have worked with people with disabilities or who have researched and/or interviewed people with disabilities. Young adult novels that have both a protagonist and an author with a disability do exist, but they're relatively rare. Like her protagonist, Harriet McBryde Johnson, the author of *Accidents of Nature*, also used a wheelchair and needed help eating, bathing, and using the bathroom. The novel is set in 1970 and takes place over the ten days that Jean attends "Camp Courage," a summer camp run by "normals" for young people with a variety of disabilities. The notes about the author in the back of the book tell us that Johnson also attended "a cross-disability summer camp." Johnson was an attorney, like Sara, the rebellious instigator in the novel, who has such an influence on Jean and the others and whose letter in the Epilogue, thirty years after the novel's summer story, is written on attorney letterhead.

Through Jean's perspective, and through the sometimes merciless tutelage of Jean's cabin mate Sara, we learn much. Those readers who do not use wheelchairs get some small sense of what that must be like. But that's beside the point. What all readers learn from this book is the folly and cruelty of one group of people trying to foist their values onto another group, pressuring them to live their lives according to the assumptions of a mainstream society that is both ignorant and arrogant. Through Jean's gradually widening perspective, we see the disabling consequences of those assumptions, as well as Sara's organized rebellion against them.

This rebellion is a hugely significant aspect of this novel: that the disabled campers assert their agency. Right under the noses of the counselors, Sara organizes in secret a "reverse telethon" for the show to parents and benefactors at the end. Through Sara's leadership, they secretly plan and successfully present, on visitors' day, this skit which makes bitter fun of the ableist myths on which some telethons—and Camp Courage—are based. These campers reject the slots they've been put into. Stepping out of the roles others have assigned them, they take control.

In this novel, as in many YA novels, there is a show, or contest, or big game at the end—a climax in which the maturing young person usually triumphs against the odds, comes out a winner, and is finally accepted into the world to which he or she wishes to belong.[2] This novel's show, the rebellion that is Sara's reverse telethon, is not at the very end—things happen in its aftermath. And the results of the powerful skit are mixed. The show is triumphant for the players, but it leaves the audience cold. Because their beliefs are so different from those of the actors, the audience members don't really get the joke, though they know they're being mocked, and Sara gets in a lot of trouble for it. Jean takes part in the skit, which is a turning point for her, but she is still processing changes and finding her identity.

In this case, the campers transform what is supposed to be a celebration of camp life, performed for the benefit of the parents and benefactors, to a powerful critique of camp life. The "reverse telethon" skit they do is so over the top that Sara, its author and organizer, is invited never to return to camp unless she signs a statement that she will forever refrain from "inappropriate" behavior. In the end, though, the world view of the audience is so different from that of transformed campers that nothing changes, and, in fact, the audience didn't really "get" what the skit was doing.

There's a scene in the British sitcom/farce, "The IT Crowd," where the two computer nerds play a practical joke on their tech-clueless office manager, Jen. They write the speech for a presentation she must give to the company. They tell her they've made arrangements for her to borrow "The Internet" for her presentation, and they give her a black, shoe-box-like object with a flashing red light on top to unveil dramatically in front of the audience. The nerds sit in the audience in eager anticipation of Jen making a fool of herself when she reveals "The Internet" to the group. But when she does so, the audience gasps in awe at Jen's visual aid, and the nerds are left mystified and disappointed. The audience is so ignorant that they don't get the joke.

Sara's bitterly ironic "reverse telethon" skit at Camp Courage has a similar reception. Sara explains:

> So here I come...thinking I could put on a reverse telethon and, symbolically at least, pull it all down. But I didn't even make a crack. Yeah, sure, they didn't know what hit them—because they didn't get hit! (215)

Like the TV audience for "The IT Crowd," however, we as readers of this novel do "get it." We as readers learn, along with Jean, to see the injustice that Sara sees.

Jean begins the summer thinking of herself as "normal." Unlike the other campers, Jean has always attended a "normal" school. When Sara, who is to begin her first year in such a school in September, says to her, "Maybe you can give me some lessons on how to be a Crip in Norm school," Jean says, "I don't think of myself as crip-pled. I'm like eve-ry-one else" (18). Sara responds: "Aw, come on. You're a Crip. Otherwise you wouldn't be in Crip Camp. Say it loud, 'I'm crippled and proud!'" (19). It takes the whole novel for Jean to really transform her thinking about who she is and how CP shapes her identity, but early in her stay at the camp, she begins to have questions about what she's always thought: "Would I be the same person without CP? My parents always say CP doesn't matter. I am just like a normal girl. But I wonder" (30). By day nine, Jean says, "a Crip is what I am" (200).

This transformation in Jean is not immediate, but there are early signs that she is ready for a radical change in her identity. She shows up to camp on the first day wearing "a culotte suit in a funny print—the words NO NO NO NO NO repeated all over" (6). On that first day, the counselor Sue speaks mostly to Jean's parents, not to Jean. On the way to the cabin, Sue natters on without interacting much with Jean, who tells us, "She doesn't give me time to talk. Maybe she thinks I can't" (8). Jean is well aware of these slights she's receiving, but she swallows her anger: "The one-sided conversation doesn't bother me. She means well" (8).[3] Even on the first day, Jean also seems to understand that Sara's name calling is not malicious. When Jean tosses her suitcase on her cot, Sara remarks, "Not bad, Spazzo" (21). The counselor, Sue, "gives her a stern look, but I'm not offended" (22).

In the early days of her stay, though, Jean's descriptions of her fellow campers are graphic and distant. She sees them through an ableist perspective, not as individuals. Later, the young woman Jean refers to as "the eyebrow tapper" will become "Mary." Dolly, who has cerebral palsy, is described as "the worst CP I've ever seen" (10). At first, Jean can't follow what Dolly is saying: "She's talking CP talk. I can't understand at all" (8). By midway through the novel, through Jean's narration, we're getting direct quotations from Dolly, so obviously Jean has learned to understand Dolly's speech. The face of Robert, the "aussie" (autistic person), becomes "human to an extreme. It is the face of a person intensely preoccupied" (44). And Jean gradually begins to see "Hideous Willie" (43) in a different way. Earlier she describes Willie as "an explosion of ugliness" (11). Later, when he sits down beside her to listen to a story, Jean thinks, "The top of his head, covered with wavy brown hair, doesn't look bad at all" (55). Jean is beginning to understand Sara's view of Willie, who has known him much longer. Sara says, "Now I almost think he's beautiful, because he looks like Willie and no one else in the world" (48).

The "NO NO NO NO NO" pattern on Jean's outfit that first day of camp parallels something that happens later. Robert, the "aussie," has not yet spoken at camp. One day, the counselors are trying to get him to go into a canoe, and he doesn't want to go. From a distance away, Jean hears from the direction of the lake "a howl of rage":

> "Noooo," it bellows. No. No. No. No." It gets louder. Now it's unmistakable; It's the aussie. Robert. We listen. I think I hear Norm calls of alarm, but they're just background noise, static, overpowered by the roar of Robert's rage." (104)

Robert finally yells out, "I AIN'T GONNA RIDE IN NO FUCKING CANOE!" (104)

The counselors are outraged, but Sara and the other campers are jubilant at Robert's rebellion. This is a significant moment for Robert, and also for Jean. She wants to tell her parents about this story, but she knows they won't see it the way she does, as "a beautiful story of a precious revelation, a marvel" (106). The next day, when Sara is offered a canoe ride, she refuses to go, and no one give her any argument. She says to Jean, "Robert's rebellion has hege-mony walking on eggs" (121).

Accidents of Nature explicitly challenges several commonplaces—taken-for-granted but unproven beliefs—about how the world works. This novel counters the ableist myth that people with impairments have no in-terest in sex or are incapable of it. In the novel's most disturbing scene, on the camp's dance floor, the able-bodied counselors tease the campers sexu-ally. Sara and Jean watch what's going on and are disgusted. Sara says, "You know, the crazy thing is not just that I can't figure out why they do it, but I can't even decide what's worse. To be so misunderstood that they don't know we're sexual? To be thought so pitiful as to need this kind of therapy? Or to be exploited for their kicks? Can you tell me what's worse?" (95).

Another ableist commonplace is the reverence for walking: that heaven and earth must be moved so that a person can get up on his or her legs and am-bulate. In this book, there are several sections where that view is questioned. Jean is at the lake beach one day and sees a boy who takes his artificial legs off to go into the water:

> Here's a boy I've seen before. I took him for a walkie-talkie in the lodge yesterday. Now he sits on a towel, disconnects both legs, and drops them on the ground. At first glance, what's left of him looks like half boy, literally truncated, a wartime fatality, you'd think. But then I watch him cross the sand on his rump and two strong arms. Free of the weight of fake legs, he speeds into the water … . (35)

A little later in the day, after Jean gets back to the cabin from the lake, Sara asks to look at Jean's photo album. As a child, Jean was a poster child for her local telethon. Sara is looking at the photo album and reading aloud to Mar-gie, another camper, some of the many newspaper clippings about Jean. We see the beginnings of Jean's transformation at the camp in this early scene: Sara is making bitter fun of the poster-child-telethon Jean, but Jean is not angry: "'Gracious peace!' Sara says. 'The Crosstown Cripple sure gets a lot of press! Who's your agent?' She's mocking me, but I don't mind" (39).

The conversation continues, and the three girls discuss the world's obses-sion with walking. This section, worth quoting at length, shows Jean—and readers—a different perspective on walking:

> She stops at a full-page story, "Crosstown Girl Learns to Walk." In the photo, I'm seven years old, adorable, with an enormous grin. I'm standing in full leg braces, my hands squeezing a walker. Sara reads it aloud, the whole story: four years of physical therapy, two operations, the high cost of keeping a growing child in braces. Proud

parents. Courage and determination. "This little girl is an inspiration" is what my physical therapist said.

She looks at me with gravity. "It looks like a good part of your childhood was swallowed up with all this walking stuff." She pauses. I shrug. (39).

Sara continues. Although Sara's rants can sometimes feel like a bit too much preaching, they are necessary for Jean to hear, and for some of us readers:

It is funny. Therapists, teachers, relatives—everyone—they all think walking is such a wonderful thing. And we don't question that. We believe it must be worthwhile, or they wouldn't torture us for it. And then, finally, you get up on your feet, take a few halting steps—pardon me, I mean courageous and determined steps—and the cameras flash, and everyone's inspired. But then you find out walking is a lousy way to move from place to place. And as you get bigger, it's worse. When you fall down, you have further to go. When you start to think for yourself, you realize a wheelchair is a better way to get where you're going. (39–40)

The girls go on to discuss particularly painful physical therapy sessions and surgeries. Near the end of this discussion, Jean is beginning to question the assumptions she's always held, that anything can be accomplished if we "just try harder," and that walking is always the ultimate goal. She thinks to herself:

Can a wheelchair be a choice, and not a failure? I'm not sure. Maybe Sara was abused by her physical therapist; surely for most people it makes sense to try to become as normal as possible. But what if normal isn't the only way to be? It's an oddly thrilling idea, but I'm not ready to put it into words. (41).

Jean's questioning of "norms" is further stimulated by rebellious antics of her cabin mates. When the campers are serenaded by the Sand Hills Community Youth Chorale, Sara and her crew know what's coming: songs whose lyrics deliver the usual Camp Courage view of its campers as tragic, sorrowful people who must be encouraged to always try harder and demonstrate non-stop courage. When the choir director introduces "The Impossible Dream," from *Man of La Mancha*, a song regularly sung to "inspire" these campers, Sara groans and calls it "The Ideal Cripple's Code of Conduct." She and some other characters are sick of its lyrics about him fighting unbeatable foes, bearing burdens, and fighting courageously. As the choir sings, Sara and some of the other campers, Willie and Margie, lip-sync the words in mockery and act out its lines in broad, comic hostility toward its ableist message. The counselors try to stop "the mirth that spreads," but they cannot. Jean observes all this, but this early in the summer, she is not ready to join in this mini-rebellion. In fact, she's not ready to even get it: "By the time Willie stands on tip-toe to reach for the unreachable star, Willie, Sara, and Margie have reached a state of high hilarity. I just can't see what's so funny" (68).

The next song, Rodgers and Hammerstein's "You'll Never Walk Alone," also meant to be inspiring, sets the group off even more with its ironic double meaning for Sara and Jean in their wheelchairs. Sara and her gang wait for the ending, "Walk on, walk on…" and the last line about never walking alone:

> Willie takes Sara's hands and my hands and joins them in his own. With death-sentence solemnity, he speaks the next line: "You'll never walk alone."
>
> Sara ham-acts a face of great distress, a face hearing very bad news for the first time.
>
> Willie sings loud, right in our faces. "You'll NEVER WALK alone!"
>
> I laugh. (70)

Jean's laughter is a turning point for her. She's beginning to realize, she tells us, "that walking is something you can mock" (70). Sara's and the others' mocking of deeply held beliefs about walking gets Jean thinking differently about the stories she read as a child:

> I am in Sunday school: "You can do it if you believe." I see Jesus cleansing lepers, giving sight to the blind, making the lame walk. He heals them all and then leaves them behind. In the fresh air of the Swiss Alps, the orphan girl Heidi tells her crippled cousin, Clara, "You can do it; just try." In the fresh air of a secret garden, another orphan girl, another crippled cousin: "You can do it; just try." As a child I loved these stories; they speak to the fundamental optimism of childhood. Part of me still believes them, or wants to. But now I yearn for a Bible story about a cripple who isn't cured. (73–74).

This counter-hegemonic view of walking is similar to other counter-hegemonic views in this novel and in disability studies. In her excellent analysis of different philosophers' views of disability, Cynthia Lewiecki-Wilson juxtaposes different views of the constructed terms "normal" and "independence," two terms deeply woven into the privileging of walking that Jean is just beginning to question in the scene just described.

Drawing on philosopher Eva Kittay (and also referencing the Prologue to *Accidents of Nature*), Lewiecki-Wilson discusses the concept of "interdependence" as opposed to the culturally constructed idealization of "independence." In the same way the character Sara questions the universal goal of walking, Kittay questions the universal goal of "independence." For her, *inter*dependence is a more valuable goal, and a more realistic way of viewing reality for everyone. As Lewiecki-Wilson puts it: "Kittay is interested in developing a more positive, complex concept of dependency than merely the negative value it carries under classical liberal theory" (90).

By the time Jean's parents pick her up to return home, she has developed a complex, nuanced view of herself and of terms like "normal." She has also found a new identity, which comes with many emotions: As Jean and her family drive away from the summer camp, she can't stop crying:

> I am howling, howling like a baby, or not really like a baby, but like the grown-up spazzo-gone-amok that I am. The sobs have a will of their own, a will that won't submit to mine. I give up the battle and let go. (222)

Jean started the summer as a naturally optimistic person. These ten days at Camp Courage have destroyed that "automatic optimism," but she has gained a kind of long-term, deeper hope. "In its place I feel the seed of a different kind of hope, a heart that knows what rage is like and trust that lives with open eyes" (223). She sees new possibilities for herself:

> I'm not sure how, exactly, but I'm pretty sure I can do it. I think I can be happy, at least as happy as most people are....One thing, however, I believe is almost certain: I'll never be 'just like a normal girl.' What I will be is beyond my imagining." (223)

She knows that she is loved by her family, but that they will not ever be able to truly understand her: "I am going on a path of my own, a road they cannot take. I'll be alone, a separate person, even if, physically, I remain as close to them as ever" (223). In the last paragraph of the novel, she says, "I have never felt more alone. I have never felt farther separated from my family. And in my whole life I have never loved them so much." (224)

Although in the beginning Jean is in a liminal position, belonging yet not belonging to her family and to the "normal" school she attends during the year, her friend Sara very clearly sees herself as a person out to challenge conventional views of disability. Sara has embraced her identity as a person who uses a wheelchair, and she cheerfully calls her fellow campers names that would shock the outside world ("spazzo," "ugly," etc.). The others know her, however, and joke themselves about their disabilities. By the end, Jean, too, is calling herself "spazzo." This is a complex situation, especially, perhaps, for some readers who are themselves "Norms." In the book, the "norms" are the oppressors, the ones who "don't get it," the ones who, even those with good intentions, patronize, insult, and sometimes even abuse the campers. It's not an easy book to read. In fact, although it is categorized as a YA novel, it's really more of an adult novel with a young adult narrator and mostly young adult characters.

It's also a highly literary novel. By that I mean that it has many textual features that appear in other novels considered artistic or literary. The dialogue is crisp and sharp. Speech tags, sometimes annoyingly overdone in lesser novels, both YA and adult, are spare and unobtrusive. There are sections of extensive, rich description, which are integral to the theme and tone of the novel, but also poetic in their own right. The Prologue describing the land on which Camp Courage is built, with its twisted, "unrehabilitated" (3) trees, the accidental survivors of neglect and harsh environment, is an extended metaphor that reappears, with a light touch, throughout the book. As Lewiecki-Wilson points out, variation in the trees that survive is one of this novel's themes (77), consistent with the wider questioning and defining of "normal" that it seems to promote.

There is also much sensory imagery, never overdone, and frequently kinesthetic descriptions that perhaps only a person in a wheelchair would be aware of. As Jean rolls over the paved paths through the woods, she describes the sensation:

> The asphalt makes the ride nice and smooth. It's so quiet I think I can hear our axles ringing, two faint notes in odd harmony with each other and with the song of a distant bird. The bird goes quiet and stillness surrounds us. We roll forward. Our damp skin breaks through the wall of air that was undisturbed until we came. (19)

So the perspective is something many "norm" readers would have never felt themselves.

If this novel were to be discussed in a book club or classroom, it's important that the discussion be framed in a way that the very stereotypes this book is challenging are not reinscribed. For example, Sara's semi-affectionate name calling could be misinterpreted. Coming from Sara, who wants her fellow campers to celebrate their individuality and identity, the words mean one thing in the context of this camp. Jean, even early in the novel seems to sense this: "She's mocking me, but I don't mind" (39). But suppose "norms" were to hurl these names at Jean and the others in a different context—in a high school hallway, for example? Those same epithets would have quite a different meaning and quite a different motivation. It's possible that young readers steeped in ableist assumptions might interpret Jean's acceptance of Sara's name calling as permission to use those names in a school yard. Teachers or other discussion leaders might pose questions designed to help casual readers understand how Sara's relationship to Jean and the other campers is very different from the average "norm's" relationship to Jean and other people with disabilities. When researching how this book was received, I found a number of positive reviews, but no "study guides" or questions to be posed about it. This suggests that *Accidents of Nature* is not widely read or discussed, either in book clubs or in schools. It should be.

The Acorn People

The audacity of Johnson's novel's counter-hegemonic stance can best be measured by juxtaposing it to another book, *The Acorn People*, by Ron Jones, with its setting also a camp for young people with disabilities. Each book has a very different message about agency, especially when comparing the culminating action in both: the show. Written in 1976 and described as based on a true story, *The Acorn People*, is a short (80 page) narrative about author Ron Jones' summer as a counselor at a camp for severely disabled children. While the children do learn some things about themselves, it is mostly Ron's awakening story. This book was and is widely read in the schools, unlike Johnson's book, which, if Google hits are seen as evidence, is not well known. There are a number of very positive reviews of *Accidents* online, including one at *Disability Studies Quarterly* (Cummins) and several at Goodreads. But if teachers are using *Accidents* in their classrooms, they are not posting their materials about it on the web.

In contrast, there are all sorts of reception documents, spanning over thirty years, on *The Acorn People*: discussion guides, vocabulary lists, quizzes, lesson plans, flashcards, and a Webquest made by seventh graders. There is also a 1981 TV movie based on this novel, staring Ted Bessell, Cloris Leachman, and LeVar Burton. It is safe to say that many more people have read and discussed *The Acorn People* than have read and discussed *Accidents of Nature*. It is still widely read in schools today. It's important, therefore, that whatever oppressive societal habits *Acorn* critiques should be foregrounded, and whatever oppressive assumptions it may perpetuate, even unintentionally, should also be foregrounded—and challenged. It's also important that Johnson's book, a tour de force of effective critique, be read and discussed way more often than it is.

Jones' book, like Johnson's, does question, though to a much different degree, the status quo regarding the treatment of disabled people. For 1976, it is quite critical, in parts, of ableist assumptions, though it doesn't use that word. It also displays several problematic assumptions typical of its time, which, if discussed in a book club or classroom, should be examined critically.

Acorn is written in a much simpler prose than is *Accidents*, is aimed at a younger audience, and is much shorter. It was also written three decades earlier, from the first-person perspective of a young man who does not identify as disabled. Except for the brief Prologue in *Accidents*, these two stories begin the same way, with the campers being dropped off by their parents. The chapters in both are named according to the duration of the stay at camp (Day One, Day Two, etc.). There are craft days in both, with generic camp projects foisted on campers by clueless directors. Just as Jean was frustrated with babyish or absurd craft projects, Ron, the young camp counselor, sees the imposed recreational schedule as oppressive: "It was a masterful plan, for scoutmasters. For us, it was out of the question" (24).

Each book culminates in a rebellion against the camp's management, and in each case the campers' behavior is described by the management as "inappropriate" (*Accidents*) or "unruly" (*Acorn*). The agents of the rebellion are very different, however. In *Acorn*, counselor Ron or the nurse are the instigators of the action, though the children do join in. In *Accidents*, significantly, it is the campers who rebel, and they must work in secret, with the counselors excluded from the plan.

Unlike Jean, the narrator and camper with cerebral palsy in *Accidents*, Ron, the narrator in *The Acorn People*, is a non-disabled counselor describing his experiences working at Camp Wiggan. As Eve Tal points out, there is a danger in having someone "in a caretaker status" narrate a story: "When outsiders write about another culture/group, they risk perpetuating stereotypes and inadvertently conveying inaccurate information" (2). The author of *Accidents* was herself disabled, used a wheelchair, and had a number of the same physical needs as Jean, whose personal perspective readers obtain in this novel. While *Accidents* is mostly Jean's finding-her-identity story, *The Acorn People* is Ron's awakening story. Jean starts camp thinking of herself as just a "normal" girl who has CP. At the end of the ten days, she claims a new identity with new possibilities. It is a complex realization for her. It separates her from her parents, but it is also exciting.

Ron begins by seeing the children at the camp as "other," as different from himself. Although on the first day he speaks of the campers as "beings without visible life" and "this mass of injury" (2), by day two he is describing each child individually by name and personality. He makes acorn necklaces with them and by page 15 "we all had this crazy nut necklace in common," and then "...we became the Acorn People" (16). As depicted in the developing narrative, the campers and counselors alike are all in this together—this being the rebellion against the camp's restrictive policies.

As the narrative develops, Ron moves from an "us/them" view to "we":

> Like it or not, we became the Acorn People. My fellow travelers and I were now drawn together like blood brothers. We would share a common history and fate. We would endure together. (16)

In the beginning, though, he pities them—something they neither wish for nor welcome—and he also lumps them all together. As he watches the children arrive, he describes them not as individuals but as a passive group, "these wheelchair children" (1), or "this mass of humanity" (4), who "all looked alike" (4) and "who move toward you only by the energy of their parents' insistence" (1). By the end of the first day the narrator has many negative emotions, including the fear that associating with them will make him like them:

> A fear emerged in my mind that this illness surrounding me would somehow rub off. That if I touched a disfigured limb or body, I could be poisoning myself. In a nightmare I dreamed of children's legs and heads unscrewing. Parts of bodies coming off in my hands. (7–8)

Seen in retrospect, through several decades of disability studies activism and rhetorical analysis, readers today will see his use of the word "illness" here as problematic. He's also using it very broadly. While some campers do have chronic or progressively debilitating illnesses, others are wheelchair users or blind, not "ill," even by 1976 definitions.

But the narrator here at least exposes a fear. He names it and puts it on the table, an admission not heard often in our society, even today. Ron admits to this ableist, perhaps unconscious, fear of contagion, a distancing, harmful emotion that may be partly responsible for the ignorant, hostile culture that disables people more than does their disability. Both books expose and critique disabling elements of this culture, though to very different degrees.

The Acorn People uses more pathos than does *Accidents of Nature*. While *Accidents* is graphic, *Acorn* is pathetic, at least in spots. While *Accidents* ends with Jean experiencing both a strange distance from her loving family and a hopeful excitement about the future, Acorn ends with the news that "All the principal children in this story are now dead" (80). *Acorn* is also more romantic and "feel good," in the sense that Ron bonds so quickly with the campers, and counselors and campers alike work together in harmony against the camp administration.

In both books, swimming is a freeing activity. In *Accidents*, Jean describes the water as "a place where the lackings of legless creatures are unimportant" (35). In the lake, she has an independence she doesn't have on land:

> I go forward until the water grabs my life vest and yanks me up. My feet lose contact with the earth, and, shivering with the wonderful cold, I lie back. The boy counselor lets go. At first he stays close enough to touch me; then he lets me drift and I am off, floating on my own" (36).

In Camp Wiggan's pool, Ron describes a similar effect of water on swimmers. Interestingly, even by this early point in the narrative, he is speaking of "our bodies" —both the campers and the counselors:

> The swimming pool was a new world for everyone. The water gave buoyancy and freedom to our bodies and to the pent up children in all of us. Each child was given an orange safety belt and carefully lifted into the pool. That's where the careful and restricted movement ended and the teasing, splashing, racing began. Children and counselors held in bondage to chairs and harnesses were free. It was as if the water gave us permission to push each other and not just be pushed. (16–17)

In some ways, this book reflects elements of U.S. culture in the 1970s. It was clearly influenced by the *we're-all-in-this-together, let's-all-be-free-and-love-the-universe* ethos. Ron describes, un-ironically, the effects of the song Cum Ba Ya (62):

> Why can't life be like this? Human beings in all their magnificence. Working to find that moment of pride. That one second of excellence at being alive. Hearing our singular voice held in harmony by the voices of those we love. The feeling of belonging not just to oneself but to the entire universe. (62)

In our present century, it's impossible to mention Cum Ba Ya without giggling. The song has become a laugh line for those wishing to make fun of any counterculture position perceived as naïve or unrealistic. And this book has some such positions. There's a hippie-era rebellion against The Man, in this case Mr. Bradshaw, the camp's director, whose assumptions and policies oppress not only the campers but somehow the counselors as well. There's also a '70s era celebration/declaration of a oneness with nature, as in this description when they reach the top of the mountain after an exhausting climb: "He gently gave the mountain one of his necklaces. Not the act of a conqueror, but a friend. We had done it" (40).

Accidents has a much different approach and is far more critical of, and bitter about, society's ableist practices. Jean, the first person narrator, is a disabled young woman attending "Camp Courage" for the first-time. In the beginning, it is Jean who sees her fellow campers as "other." By the end of the novel, she feels separate from her family—though she still loves them—and she bonds with Sara, Willie, and the others, who proudly claim their Crip identity. The counselors in *Accidents* are not, like in *Acorn*, allies and fellow rebels. In this novel, the counselors are clearly "other," the "Norms" who don't get it.

Another ableist myth both books critique—again, to different degrees—is that people with disabilities are not interested in sex, or ought not to be. In *Acorn*, Ron seems to see this myth being enforced and to reject it at the same time. Fairly early in the narrative, he critiques the separation of boys and girls:

> …this carousel schedule kept the kids from meeting other kids. You were always with the same group. This meant boys and girls were never together. Oh, perhaps that was the reason for all this. (25)

In the next sentence, he proposes to the whole group of boys that they go to the pool right after breakfast, instead of sticking to the director's schedule. They all agree. The girls are using the pool when the boys arrive, and what Ron describes next is a direct challenge to ableist assumptions regarding sex:

> Participants in this first-ever "integrated swim" were self-conscious and then flirtatious in a typically pubescent way….Soon, like melting ice cream, the sun and water worked their magic. Children—no, young adults, no, children—were playing the games of dunk and run or just plain show-off. With coy glances and gossipy chatter, the girls attracted the boys' attention. The boys relied on stunts of bravery to claim equal attention….They were playing bumper cars [in their inner tubes] in a soft but deliberate way. It was almost erotic. (25–26)

Ron then says this: "All my questions about sex and the handicapped were answered in front of my gaze. If ever there was a dance of affection, with taunts and prowess and just plain sexual play, it was taking place in the splashes and noise before me" (26). That Ron *has* questions "about sex and the handi-capped" establishes the fact of this myth's existence in our culture. (Would a counselor at a "normal" camp bother to remark upon boys and girls flirting with one another?) But though it's offensive to see the starkness of this myth in Ron's observations, this section also puts the myth on the table so that it can be named, discussed, and challenged.

Both books also have scenes where the counselors interact with the camp-ers in an improper way, sexually. In *Accidents*, Sara and the others are appalled by the behavior of some of the counselors at the dance, who tease the campers sexually in ways that are both unseemly and cruel. We view this disturbing scene through the outraged perspective of Jean and Sara. In *Acorn*, when the campers are going home, Ron kisses a young girl, Mary, who has had a crush on him. This action (kissing her on the lips) is not depicted as inappropriate, but as a gentle, "unexpected moment" that would make Ron "remember sum-mer camp forever." He believes the other members of the "Acorn Society" are okay with him kissing the camper: "I think they knew and even approved" (79). But then, this was the '70s, the villain role is safely assigned to Mr. Bradshaw, the camp director, and Ron is also narrating this story. However, any discussion of *Acorn* today should foreground this scene for discussion and critique, especially if the discussants are students, summer campers, teachers, counselors, or anyone who has anything to do with children.

Both books also occasionally critique the physical inaccessibility of their respective camp. Although Jean's Camp Courage does have paved paths so that people using wheelchairs can enjoy the trails through the woods (19), Camp Wiggan has no such amenities. Even on that first day, Ron sees that the camp, usually inhabited by Boy Scouts, is not accessible to the very people who are now paying to go there. He's also clearly not received any training for his counselor position at this camp:

> Each cabin had three steps. Steps that became hurdles. You can't wheel a chair straight up a set of stairs. I tried that with one kid and spilled him head first. Every-thing had to be learned. The simplest task was an ordeal. (6)

He also says, "I was silently cursing toilets that didn't have grab bars." (6). Later, as the counselors work to get the children up and dressed, Ron complains: "The cabin is very confining. Definitely not built for wheelchairs" (22). In 1976, to have a popular school book critiquing the lack of wheelchair space, ramps, and grab bars was rare. It still is.

Although there is a rebellion against ableist-driven assumptions and activities in both books, the critical difference between them is one of agency: who initiates the action against the oppressive authority. In *Acorn*, Ron, the counselor, and also Mrs. Nelson, the nurse, take turns being the main agents of action, though the children join in and expand the action, becoming secondary agents. It is Ron who makes the first acorn necklace, which "wasn't a designated project" (14–15). But it is Benny B, one of the campers, who takes off with the idea, saying, "we're all a little nutty here!" (15). Spider, another child, joins in to say, "We're the Acorn People," and then Ron calls everyone, "my fellow travelers," the "Acorn People" (16). Later, the counselors, the nurse, and the campers all join together against a common enemy, Mr. Bradshaw, the camp director, who forces the children into regimented, boring activities hatched from a variety of ableist assumptions. When campers and counselors alike are frustrated with the lockstep recreational schedule set by Mr. Bradshaw, Ron and his fellow counselors come up with the plan to change it, though they do consult with the campers and take a vote:

> Dominic and I decided at breakfast to talk with the kids about the day ahead as if we could plan it ourselves. Following breakfast we would go directly to the pool. The decision was unanimous. (25)

On Day 6, it is Benny B, one of the campers, who suggests another activity that would not have been approved by Mr. Bradshaw, climbing a mountain. He says, "If the Boy Scouts can climb that mountain, can we?" (29). "Day 6" is a long, dramatic chapter, clearly meant to be inspiring, that describes some children pushing each other's wheelchairs, and others eventually abandoning their wheelchairs to scootch up the mountain by sitting down and pushing themselves backwards. Finally, after much effort, they all make it to the summit. Seen from almost 40 years later, it's hard to know whether to view this mountain climbing as the children's triumphant departure from what the administration views as proper, or as a capitulation to "normal" society's exhortation to "just try harder." Are the children rebelling against what society thinks is good for them, or have they merely internalized the "climb every mountain" cliché so despised and ridiculed by Sara, Willie, Margie, and eventually Jean in *Accidents*?

It's also hard to say, definitively, what cultural work (Jane Tompkin's phrase) *Acorn* accomplishes. Does it challenge or support harmful ableist myths? Does it do both? The children's desire to climb the mountain, and to do it by literally leaving their wheelchairs behind, might play to the same "courage and determination" assumptions that *Accidents* skewers so effectively. The "ultimate victory" (40) of the literal mountain climbing in *Acorn* and the "unexpected strength" (41) the children need to haul themselves up the mountain inch by inch contrasts starkly with the scene in *Accidents* where Sara, Willie, and the others make such bitter fun of the lyrics the Youth Chorale sing at them every year, with its "climb every mountain" message. It's possible that the children in *Acorn* are subconsciously playing out the "keep-trying-no-matter-what" commonplaces in the "Man of La Mancha" song, which Sara in *Accidents* dubs "The Ideal Cripple's Code of Conduct" (68).

Mr. Bradshaw, of course, does not approve of this mountain climbing activity or any of the other "unruly behavior" that's been going on, and he puts a stop to it for a while, until there is another rebellion, a tearing down of the labels he had ordered. It is the drunk camp nurse, the beloved Mrs. Nelson, "who suddenly refuses to let her children be condemned to a label" (55) and initiates this literal and figurative elimination of labels. The counselors and campers finish the job. It is Mrs. Nelson, too, who proposes the rebellious and unconventional "Camp Wiggan Water Extravaganza," which casts the children not as observers but as participants. The setting for the show is a "rogue pirate ship," possibly symbolic of the anti-authoritarian stance the show will promote. The children agree to it instantly, even ask to do it, but they are not the agents. Mrs. Nelson plans it all, assuring them that all they need do "is listen carefully and follow my instructions" (69). The message here is that these children need outside help to assert themselves and that they cannot do it unassisted. The parents and siblings in this book are delighted by the show, obviously approving of its anti-authoritarian message, and Mr. Bradshaw conveniently arrives on the scene too late to stop it. Except for the sad epilogue that informs us that "All the principal children in this story are now dead," (80), the book more or less ends with the triumphant splashing and interaction of the children, which transforms them and the counselors as well.

In *Accidents*, it is the fed up campers, led by Sara and joined finally by Jean, who rebel against directors and counselors alike. In *Acorn*, counselor and narrator Ron uses "we" to refer to both campers and the now enlightened counselors. In *Accidents*, camper and narrator Jean at first sees herself as different and separate from the other campers, the "eyebrow tappers and babblers and all kinds of strange people..." (17). In discussing Butner, a school seen as a place "for the criminally insane and mentally retarded" (16), a place the family doctor had advised her parents to send her, Jean thinks, "I'm not the kind of person who goes to Butner" (17). But by the time she leaves Camp Courage, she says this about Sara and the camp: "I'll never be like Sara, but I don't have to be. With her, I can be myself. Even become myself. To become myself, I need this place, this strange place, whether I like it or not" (217).

Although *The Acorn People* does call into question some ableist myths about sex, self-determination, and individuality, it also reflects some troublesome assumptions. While the campers do participate, quite actively, in planning the new activities, tearing down the insulting labels, and acting in the pirate show at the end, it is the nurse or the counselors who initiate the first steps of each rebellion. Unlike *Accidents*, which critiques the whole of society for its patronizing, de-humanizing assumptions about people with disabilities, *Acorn* makes Mr. Bradshaw the scapegoat for all that is evil, leaving the rest of society off the hook and showing counselors, staff, and parents all fully supportive and in cahoots with the children. The main difference in the rebellion is agency. Long-time camper Sara leads the action in *Accidents*. New counselor Ron leads the action in *Acorn*.

In some ways, the two books are apples and oranges. One is a novel (with some auto-biographical elements) published in 2006 (but set in 1970); the other is a narrative based on a true story, published in 1976. But *Accidents'* blistering critique, read by itself, especially if it is the first novel young people might read about disabilities, might be too much for some "norms" to read and digest. And *Acorn*, read by itself, might inadvertently perpetuate harmful stereotypes about which groups are capable of asserting agency in their own lives—though it may also be an important "awakening" story for some readers. It will only take them so far, however. That is why it may be important to read the two books together, say, in a book club or classroom, so that any latent, harmful assumptions that exist in readers about whether disabled people are capable of speaking up and acting on their own behalf can be challenged. *Acorn* is effective to a certain degree: it shows the campers as individuals, as real children with a sense of humor, sexual desire, and some degree of agency. And it contains an early critique of inaccessible buildings, rooms, and bathrooms. But *Accidents* illustrates the "Nothing About Us Without Us" (James Charlton's phrase) belief of many people in the disability studies movement. Since Harriet McBryde Johnson was a such a strong disability rights activist, this is not surprising. One almost wonders if she wrote her book as a response to *The Acorn People*.

Handling Discussions of These Books

Whether these books are read by themselves or juxtaposed with each other, it's important that discussions about them steer people away from cementing further any prejudices they might harbor. As Judith Landrum and others have pointed out, discussions before and after the reading of these texts are critical in helping students change negative views they might have of disabilities (285). On the web today, there are many "discussion questions," for example, and activities/assignments concerning *Acorn*. They, too, should be examined and critiqued.

One way to help prevent discussions of these books about disability from descending into any further cementing of ableist myths is to consider questions which encourage a more critical view of the status quo. If a book, for example, blithely incorporates a stereotype but does not call it into question, either through irony or through a character's comment on it, teachers might encourage students to become what Judith Fetterley calls "resisting readers"—to recognize and then resist a text's harmful assumptions about groups of people characterized in it. Several scholars have started such resistance. They've analyzed questions, assignments, and activities put forward about books with harmful assumptions. Their analysis is worth revisiting before suggesting discussion questions for *Acorn* or *Accidents*.

In her article, "Add Disability and Stir," which appears in *Disability and the Teaching of Writing*, Deb Martin critiques composition textbooks in which readings about disability, when they are (rarely) included, are simply "add-ons." As Lewiecki-Wilson and Brueggemann (with Dolmage) point out in their editorial introduction to Martin's piece, her research suggests that these textbooks "do not ask students to consider their own roles in constructing disability nor as possible recipients of such policies. Textbooks typically narrate from an ableist voice…." (74). Martin analyzes from a rhetorical perspective the questions and assignments created in such textbooks. But her analysis is also relevant to a discussion of young adult novels. She argues that harmful, hegemonic assumptions are sometimes embedded in such questions and assignments, in this case setting up or perpetuating an *us/them* binary that plays into such assumptions. For example, Martin foregrounds an activity suggested on page 207 of the textbook *Uncommon Threads*, in which students are asked to "'create an image text showing how *we* might revise *our* attitudes toward

the *physically* challenged'" (Martin's emphasis, 83). Martin's rhetorical analysis here is worth quoting at length:

> Intending the pronouns "we" and "our" to refer to abled-bodied [sic] people who need
> attitude adjustments, the authors make apparent not only that they are situated in
> the dominant category but that they expect that all of their readers are too. By setting
> up an us/them scenario "the physically challenged" become an essentialized group
> whose core essence is how they are treated. (83)

While the textbook activity is no doubt well intentioned and somewhat useful—implying that some people's attitudes do need to be revised if the world
is to become more inclusive—Martin's rhetorical analysis demonstrates the
binary at work in the language and why that binary can be harmful.

Martin goes on to critique other textbooks' editorial materials and the
assumptions underpinning them. A number of textbook authors, Martin says,
seem to imply that "help" for people with disabilities is what is needed. But
help, says Martin,

> is not necessarily what people with disabilities need or want, however. Ultimately,
> by asking students to solve the "dis-ability problem," the book presents dis-ability
> as someone else's need. Students are no closer to examining society's lack of ac-
> commodations or their own role in creating negative experiences for people with
> disabilities; nor are they interrogating language's role in perpetuating negative con-
> sequences. (87)

A better question, says Martin, is posed in the Webb and Thompson
Rhetorical Contexts reader. In that book's editorial introduction to one of
the essays, students are asked to examine the featured essay for words or
phrases that reveal the author's apparent assumptions about readers (89).
This is an extremely valuable task to ask students to do. Not only does it
teach them to analyze texts rhetorically; it can help them better understand the constructed nature of disability. It can also teach them valuable
inference tools, a skill often abandoned in today's emphasis on low-level,
literal reading comprehension skills required in so many standardized
assessments.

Martin's argument concerns texbooks designed for composition classrooms, and she says "no precise recipe" exists for an ideal way to include
disability in the classroom. However, her view about writing pedagogy and
disability can also be applied to discussions of disability in young adult novels:

By being more willing to recognize contradictions, power imbalances, and cultural myths associated with the construction of dis-ability, and the constraints of textbooks in their prescribed forms, we not only have the potential for more open and honest discussions, but we honor writing's function in creating and understanding knowledge. (90)

The editors of *Disability and the Teaching of Writing*, in their editorial section on "Designing Assignments" regarding Martin's article, encourage teachers to revisit their assignment design with questions inspired by Martin's argument: "Does your assignment ask students to position themselves as experts when they are not? Does your assignment too easily split us into an 'us/them' binary?" (Lewiecki-Wilson, Brueggemann, with Dolmage, 91).

Other challenging questions can be used to illuminate discussions of *Acorn* and other YA novels on disability. In their Introduction to the guest edited issue they did for *Disability Studies Quarterly* (*DSQ*) on Disability Studies in the Undergraduate Classroom, Amy Vidali, Margaret Price, and Cynthia Lewiecki-Wilson also discuss classroom assignments, especially the "before and after" reflections, which many teachers have their students write. These pieces involve "a reflection that pertained in some way to disability at the start of the semester, followed by disability-themed coursework, and a culminating reflection at the end of the semester." While there is a place for such an assignment, these editors argue, it can also become simply an "enlightenment narrative" which "reifies assumptions about 'disabled' and 'nondisabled' as rigid categories, and implies that disabled persons exist in order to serve as educational devices" (Introduction).

In her essay in that special issue, Valerie Struthers Walker describes how she wanted to challenge her students to grapple "with alternative and potential critiques of dominant medical/therapeutic discourses with which they were most familiar." One of the questions she posed in her adolescent literature class was, "How do our own experiences and beliefs shape the meanings we make of representations of disability in texts?" ("Questioning Representations..."). Such a question would push students beyond the limited "be more helpful" stance some questions invite and beyond the "disabled person as educational device" approach established by some other discussion questions. In contrast, Walker's question would help students consider the constructed nature of "disability" as well as to what extent they were participating in that construction, either as the so-called "non-disabled" or as "disabled" people who may have internalized some of society's myths about disability, as did some of these young adult characters.

Reception Documents for *The Acorn People*

With these scholars' analyses as a framework for discussion, let's look at some of the questions and activities available on the web regarding *The Acorn People*. There are many plot summaries, simplistic reading comprehension questions, flashcards with vocabulary words, and the ubiquitous, and often first, question, "What does the acorn necklace symbolize?" There are lists of questions which seem to support—perhaps unintentionally on the part of the question writers—the status quo and are problematic in the ways Martin and Vidali, Price, and Lewiecki-Wilson and others describe above. There are also other questions that seem to invite students to question the status quo.

Although there are many short lists of questions available on the web, it is unusual to find an almost two-week unit on disability: readings, activities, discussion questions, and disability-related assignments. One such unit on *Acorn* is a fairly comprehensive, 10-day lesson at NCTE's popular *Read/Write/Think* site. Designed by Krista Sherman for grades 9–12, this one is called "Inclusive Stories: Teaching About Disabilities With Picture Books."

This is a worthwhile and extensive unit, with a good mix of multisensory activities and active learning tasks. Students listen to *The Acorn People* read out loud; they read picture books on disability, do their own research, listen to presentations, discuss the texts, and then create their own picture book. Significantly, there is a plan to invite in as speakers students "who are willing to share talk about their disabilities and how they are affected by them at school." The author also encourages teachers to ask students from another class or school personnel or teachers with disabilities. She writes, "You may be surprised how many teachers have disabilities." It's important to acknowledge the normalcy of disability and to hear the perspective and voices of those who have first-hand experience with disabilities. A unit about disabilities should include the voices of those (of us) with disabilities.[4]

One of the objectives of the unit is that students will "begin to understand and appreciate the different disabilities found within your school by reading and writing about them." The students are to read a number of picture books and summarize them on worksheets. The worksheets pose questions about how the person with the disability was treated at the beginning, middle, and end of the story. Students are also asked to identify "the author's theme." The picture books the students eventually write themselves have "the purpose of teaching readers about children with various disabilities." These goals come close to the "enlightenment narrative" and "disabled persons...as educational devices" purpose Vidali, Price, and Lewiecki-Wilson warn against. These goals also may be revealing assumptions about readers in a way that inadvertently binarizes "abled" and "disabled."

Because of the far-reaching influence of our ableist culture and the limits of our language, it is extremely difficult to avoid these binaries. Even as I critique sections of Sherman's unit plan, it is important to point out how rare it is to find on the web such a detailed, well-planned lesson on disability or books about disability. Yes, some of the questions and goals fall into the traps scholars warn against, but it is still possible to use these goals and questions to challenge the status quo, as long as the teacher or discussion leader is aware of the cultural work they can do—positive and negative—and broaches these possibilities with those discussing the book.

One objective of the unit is to "Practice critical thinking by analyzing picture books about disabilities." It's not clear what Sherman means here by "critical thinking" and "analyzing picture books." If the picture books being studied, or the language in them, display any myths or stereotypical views of disability, the readers are not asked to comment on that. A question Martin highlights from one of the textbooks she studied (Webb and Thompson's *Rhetorical Contexts*) might be useful here. Students are asked to "look for evidence that the author has certain presumptions about the interests and attitudes of his readers" (qtd. in Martin, 89). While this activity is designed for college students, high school students can certainly rise to this intellectual task if the teacher models the process first, using Vygotsky's "zone of proximal development" as a guide. That is, students can accomplish increasingly higher-level tasks if they at first work with a teacher on that task. But the teacher has to have that challenging objective to begin with.

The picture books the students eventually create themselves have "the purpose of teaching readers about children with various disabilities." It's a worthwhile goal, of course, to provide accurate and up-to-date information to readers. Doing so can reduce ignorance and unhealthy curiosity. Even readers with one or more impairments may not be well informed about others. There is certainly a place for such a purpose and for questions posed about information provided in such texts. One further purpose of creating these books, but one that is not mentioned, might be to expose society's disabling barriers and try to reduce them.

However, some of the questions posed about *Acorn* in this lesson plan *can* lead readers down a more analytic path. On the first day, the teacher reads the beginning of the novel aloud for ten minutes. During that first ten-minute reading, listeners would hear Ron using unfortunate terms to refer to the campers: "these wheelchair children," "beings without visible life," and "this mass of injury." The following questions Sherman poses about these phrases invites class members to examine these terms: "How do the counselors react to the campers?" and "What do you think about the language the author uses?" Through these questions, the teacher, without preaching or lecturing, allows the class to notice problems with this language. Additional questions from this unit plan are worth analyzing: "Have you ever seen a physically disabled stranger? If so, what was your reaction and why do you think you responded that way?" The first part seems to assume that the "you" is not disabled, so physical disability is cast as different and strange. The second part, however, does invite students to look at their own behavior and try to trace what factors influenced it, thus suggesting, subtly, society's role in constructing disability.

Other online resources are worth examining. Jacqueline Starke designed a webquest for her seventh graders in which they are to design a camp for people with disabilities and then argue for their design:

The Task

As you read the book, **The Acorn People,** you will learn about people with various physical disabilities. You will become aware of the various physical limitations and adaptations persons with disabilities need.

The **Americans With Disabilities Act (ADA)** has given the state of Missouri a grant to provide funding for a new camp for disabled campers. Only one contract will be awarded and your group wants it. Your group will be responsible for designing a new camp for disabled campers. The governer [sic] of Missouri ants [sic] public input as to which design is most appropriate for the special needs of the campers. Groups must also create a web page (advertisement) campaign. Once the web page has gone live, the Missouri voters will vote on the best design. (Starke)

This is a challenging task that requires reading, analysis, thinking, and imagination. The assignment is set in a realistic rhetorical situation; the audience and purpose are clear, and students must learn and practice argumentative skills. Part of the directions warrant some comments and caveats, however. One question Starke uses to introduce the unit seems to assume that the students embarking on this assignment do not identify as disabled: "What if you didn't have any legs or were blind?" The possible harm here, as Martin has pointed out, is that such a question can teach students "that dis-ability is something that is happening 'out there' to people not like themselves" (83).

The next question, however, does set up the conditions in which students can begin to question the accessibility of conventional summer camps: "What would the camp experience be like for you?" Although it does not ask students, as Martin would like teachers to do, "to examine their own role in the social construction of dis-ability" (Starke 83), such a question does at least get students thinking about constructions like stairs, narrow doorways, etc.

Starke explains why she created this webquest: "Living in school district with very few persons with disabilities, I designed this webquest to help students learn tolerance and exercise empathy." Helping students "learn tolerance and exercise empathy" implies that there is something negative about persons with disabilities, something that must be "tolerated." After all, people are never asked to "tolerate" people with positive characteristics. "Empathy" can also have negative connotations. Starke's syntax also seems to suggest that the students who are supposed to be developing this tolerance are people who do not have any disabilities.

She also says, "This lesson was also designed to assess student reading comprehension and critical thinking." She does not elaborate on what she means by "critical thinking," so her lesson objectives and questions must help us determine that. Her concern with "student reading comprehension" is understandable and warranted, however, since K-12 teachers these days are under extremely high and constant pressure to raise student reading scores or else—the "or else" being the loss of their jobs. And the intense scrutiny is on the teachers, not on the publishing companies, who make money by both making the tests and providing practice materials for them. But that's a topic for another time.

In her conclusion to the webquest, Mrs. Starke poses some questions that do push students beyond conventional "tolerance" goals. She writes:

> Just because you weren't born with a disability doesn't mean you couldn't develop one or become disabled due to an injury or accident. How would you want to be treated? Would you have been part of The Acorn Society? Would you want to attend a camp like the one you designed? How "dis"abled are disabled people?
>
> Just some things to think about............................Mrs.Starke

The idea that anyone can develop a disability begins to break down the us/them binary that is so easy to let influence our language. Asking students to think about the design of a camp shifts the focus from what is "wrong" with an individual to what is wrong with the built environment in which that person is trying to function. Such a question could open a discussion of how a culture or society can be the primary disabler, and it could support research on universal design.

It is no doubt churlish to criticize this webquest because it is not ideal, because it does not do what it could do, or because its language in part reflects the binaries and harmful commonplaces that are so strong, yet sometimes so ubiquitous that they are invisible. Indeed, all our words, including mine, do the same thing. So I write this critique not to call Mrs. Starke to task, but to use her good work as a tool to push us all further. As stated earlier, detailed, worthwhile high school or middle school lessons on disability are not that easy to find on the web. As Martin says in her discussion of disability issues in writing pedagogy, "There is no precise recipe" (90). So although I examine Mrs. Starke's words carefully, I salute her for what, in her hands, is no doubt a challenging, informative, and critical-thinking-inducing project. In this second decade of the 21st century, when there is such a hostile attitude toward teachers, it is admirable and somewhat miraculous that teachers like Mrs. Starke take the time to develop imaginative lessons like this one on this topic.

There is another *Acorn* Reading Guide on the web, this one posted by Diana Beam, a 9th grade English teacher at Wilson Memorial High School in Fishersville, VA. In her notes on the book, this teacher says that one of the children, Benny B, "suffers from polio." Another child, Thomas Stewart, is described in her summary as "confined to a wheelchair." For years, disability activists have been trying to get people to stop using "suffers" as descriptors because such words can help perpetuate the myth that the lives of people with disability are filled only with suffering. And "confined to a wheelchair" is a similarly negative phrase, implying passivity and lack of agency. To say that a person "uses a wheelchair" communicates the same fact without the connotations of the person being trapped or imprisoned. While I applaud this teacher for drawing attention to disability issues, those surfing the web for summaries or discussion questions might wish to tweak the phrasing on any materials they adapt for their own classes.

Mrs. Beam does pose some questions for her students, however, that might lead them to a more critical examination of society's role in creating a disabling environment. She asks, "Do you think 'labeling' a person is correct?

Why or why not? In your daily life how do you 'label' or 'categorize' people?" These questions, asked in a critical context, might spark some insightful discussions. Ninth graders would be particularly sensitive to some rather cruel labeling, so these questions could push them to rethink how "abled" and "disabled" are used in our society. She also asks, "Why does the counselor feel that Camp Wiggin is an odd place for these children?" Such a question might prompt a follow-up discussion of disabling buildings and parks as well as an introduction to universal design.

Although not about *Acorn*, an article by Kurtts and Gavigan in the journal *Education Libraries* describes an interesting activity. The authors suggest that pre-service teachers read two children's literature books and then consider the following questions:

> a. How are individuals with disabilities portrayed? Pathetic, sad, to be pitied? Heroic, succeeding against all odds? Or realistically?
> b. How are relationships with non-disabled peers or adults described? (25)

These questions invite pre-service teachers to recognize and begin to critique harmful stereotypes. If teachers learn to ask these questions themselves and have a chance to practice this kind of analysis, they and their students may develop a healthy skepticism about cultural prejudices that are too easy to take for granted.

It's neither possible nor productive to sit here forever applauding or booing other people's questions and assignments related to *Acorn* or other materials on disability. My materials could—and should—receive the same scrutiny. The point of this picking apart of discussion questions is to encourage those who generate questions for their class or reading group to consider the implications of both what is asked and what is not asked and to consider whether their questions inadvertently support ableist assumptions or challenge the group to consider more inclusive, counter-hegemonic changes in society. I thank those teachers enthusiastic enough and courageous enough to put forward their classroom suggestions, activities, and assignments. Actually creating a meaningful sequence of readings, research, and discussion questions and posting them for others to see is an action that inspires the rest of us to build on their good work.

In this spirit, I offer some of my own discussion questions regarding either one or both novels, *Accidents* and *Acorn*:

- In each book, to what extent does the physical design of the camp itself disable the campers (the buildings, the bathrooms, the swimming facilities, etc.)?
- To what extent might the effects of name calling (or the use of nicknames) change, depending on context and circumstances? For example, regarding *Accidents of Nature*, describe Jean's reaction to the name calling Sara subjects her to, that is, the nicknames Sara gives to Jean and the other campers. Would Jean have had the same reaction to these names in another context?—if the name calling had come from one of her schoolmates in the "norm" school, for example, or from a stranger on the street? How do different settings and relationships between people forbid or permit the use of such names?
- *The Acorn People* is told from the point of view of Ron, one of the counselors. How might the story be different if Aaron or Mary or Benny B told it? Or Mr. Bradshaw, the director? Or Mrs. Nelson, the nurse?
- What if Sue narrated the events in *Accidents of Nature*? Or Mr. Bradshaw?
- To what extent are various individual perspectives represented? Whose perspective is most represented? Whose perspective is least represented?
- What role do dominant assumptions in society play in the extent of each person's impairment?
- What role might each reader play in how disability is viewed in society?
- What role might each reader play in limitations or opportunities for those (of us) with disabilities?

My questions and those borrowed from an online search, as well as the critiques of such questions, are offered here merely as a starting point. It is hoped that imaginative instructors interested in using these or other novels as tools for critical rhetorical analysis will choose texts challenging enough to contribute to these teachers' own carefully considered goals and objectives, and that they will design questions sophisticated enough to get beyond unthinking acceptance of an unacceptable status quo.

Notes

1. I first learned of the existence of this novel from Cynthia Lewiecki-Wilson's article in *JAC*, for which I am grateful to her.
2. I call these "Napoleon Dynamite" stories, named after the 2004 film in which the culminating scene is Napoleon's crowd-pleasing dance near the end.

3. "Meaning well" was a troublesome idea for Harriet McBryde Johnson. In her 2005 book, *Too Late to Die Young*, she writes (pages 49–54) about telethons and the harm they can do under the auspices of "meaning well."

4. The phrase, "those (of us) with disabilities," is my attempt to disrupt harmful binaries, to mitigate the categorical divide between "abled" and "disabled," and to help me address my editorial stance. My intent in using "those (of us) with disabilities" here, with the parentheses, is to suggest a third both/and category regarding these troubled terms, or at least a well-intentioned ambiguity. The phrase is meant to include both those who do claim disability status and those who do not. It is also meant to remind readers of the "normality" of disability. I do not claim disability status, though I hope I may be considered an ally.

· 2 ·

RESPECT, ETIQUETTE, AND THE DRAMA OF RUDE BEHAVIOR

Some YA novels have sections that provide subtle or not-so-subtle suggestions to non-disabled people regarding how to interact with more respect toward disabled people. For readers who know enough, for example, to face—and not turn away from—people trying to read their lips, these built-in lessons on etiquette might seem obvious. But if readers don't know, or haven't had the opportunity to think about these common courtesies, the frustrations we see, for example, through the perspective of a deaf narrator—the drama of the scene—can cement these gestures of respect and consideration in a way a lecture or textbook list of rules cannot.

Who am I to collect and judge fictional scenes on disability protocol? This is a question I keep returning to as I work on this project. As I've mentioned previously, I am not currently disabled in the way that word is commonly used. Some of the authors including such scenes are not themselves disabled. How would they know, how would I know, what is good and bad behavior, assuming there is even a general consensus on this?

I cannot judge these scenes based on my personal experience. What I can say with some authority is this: The texts I write about in this chapter are among the very few novels I've encountered that substantially address the subject of what is courteous or rude behavior toward people with disabilities, which is not to say they are the only ones that do. But I've read my share of novels, beginning with my own non-stop reading as an adolescent, as an undergraduate English (literature) major, as an English masters/doctoral student, as a high school teacher of many classic and contemporary novels, short stories, and plays, and as an instructor/professor. Since I received my doctorate in 1991, I've taught many introduction to literature or fiction courses, some women's literature and world literature courses, and some Shakespeare. Now I mostly teach courses in composition, rhetoric, English education, and young adult literature, where there is much material on disability, but not on YA fictional characters with disabilities.

Two novels that include such scenes are recent ones: *The Dark Days of Hamburger Halpin*, by Josh Berk (Alfred A. Knopf, 2010) and *Five Flavors of Dumb*, by Antony John (Penguin, 2010). Both novels feature as a first person narrator a high school student who is deaf. Both novels seamlessly address a recommended protocol, if you will, of being around people who cannot hear. Both protagonists read lips but only, of course, if the speaker is facing them. Both get annoyed at teachers, parents, or others who turn away while they are speaking. Both these narrators, one male and one female, are irreverent and human. Both give some perspective to what it's like to be deaf, especially, perhaps, *Dark Days*, because the snatches of dialogue the narrator provides from the other characters sometimes have words or phrases missing because the narrator didn't catch them in his lip reading because the speaker turned away. In both novels the "good" characters already know sign or are learning it by the end.

Dark Days

The narrator in *The Dark Days of Hamburger Halpin* is Will Halpin, a 16 year old deaf student who is also, as described on the book flap, "hefty." "Hamburger" is his texting name. The book opens with Will having just moved from a deaf school to a mainstream public school in a coal-mining area of Pennsylvania. He's left the deaf school because he's not radical enough for some of the students there; he critiques deaf identity a bit for its "infights and deaf-world arguments" (2), but it's possible that we as readers should view his critique with some skepticism. As seems to be true in a number of YA novels about disability, the mother rules the roost, and the father is cowed. However, in this book, it is also the mother who has learned sign language. She signs because she knows Will prefers it to speech. The father mumbles.

On the first day in the mainstream school, Will's history teacher, Mr. Arterberry, at first remembers the school nurse's instructions to put Will where he can read lips more easily:

> Mr. A. has a seat for me off in a corner of the room. This will allow me to read lips of teacher as well as students and thus benefit from the fantastic scholarly wisdom offered by both lecture and class discussion. But it also makes me feel shoved aside, sort of like a houseplant. Will someone at least remember to prune and water me? (7)

Before long, however, the teacher forgets that he is supposed to face Will when he speaks and that he needs to keep a sight line open so that Will can read his lips:

> Even though I have always been exceptionally good at lipreading... I need to actually see the lips.... Arterberry keeps turning around or covering his mouth with his flabby arm while writing on the board. Plus, although I realize that the Americans with Disabilities Act can't force him to get rid of his bushy lip beast, a basic sense of fashion and/or hygiene should compel him to at least trip his 'stache. (8)

Other passages seem to provide some perspective that some readers might not ordinarily have access to. The school changes classes after a bell rings. Will asks, "Would it kill them to get a strobe light to flash when class ended? Or maybe a beautiful girl who could hold up a sign for me like in boxing matches?" (28). He can't turn his lip-reading off, so at lunch, when everyone at his table is talking at once, it's a "hivelike atmosphere" for him: "It's like watching TV while someone else works the remote" (16). We also learn about Will's alarm clock "that shines a bright light and literally shakes you awake in the morning" (46).

In addition to its commentary on lipreading, *Dark Days* also critiques mainstream culture and the bad behavior of the non-deaf world. It's a good thing that Will can lip-read well because the mainstream school he's now transferring to is not well funded and lacks much of what is necessary in order to provide full inclusion:

> CHS [Carbon High School] cannot afford a cool captioning system like some of the fancy schools over the river: There are no interpreters. There's no structured "inclusion" program. What they have is pretty much "sink or swim." And from what I hear (so to sign, *not* speak), sink is the more common outcome. (2)

On Will's first day at Carbon High he meets with Principal Kroener, who is on the phone when Will enters the room. As Will waits for him to get off the phone, he reads his own Individualized Education Program (IEP) report, which is upside down on the desk.

> The fact that I require an IEP reminds me that I'm still on the banks of the main-stream. And though the sheet is upside-down from where I sit, I can make out the basics. Apparently, I'm "profoundly deaf yet intellectually capable." This *yet* pisses me off! It's the kind of thing some of my old classmates would have formed a protest committee over. (6)

The *yet*, of course, reveals the IEP writer's assumption that a person who is profoundly deaf should not be expected to be intellectually capable. Will says no more about this insult, but the point is made dramatically through Will's anger in a way that readers—perhaps even readers who might harbor similar assumptions—will also be angry at the ignorant principal. We also see Will remembering with admiration his former classmates at the deaf school and their political activism, a quality that he had critiqued only pages earlier. In the next paragraph Will tells us that "People have laughed at the way I talk…" (6). Just six pages into this narrative, we already like Will and do not want people ridiculing him.

Because Will, the first person narrator in *Dark Days*, is deaf, and the conversation of others is filtered through what he is able to lip-read, there are occasional gaps in the narrative. He mentions several times when people turn away or cover their mouths when they're speaking, which makes it impossible for him to get every word they say. These interruptions are indicated in the narrative by the parenthetical "(*something something*)" inserted into the prose. In the following passage Will is describing a classroom discussion led by his teacher, Mr. Arterberry:

> "Was there anything (*something something*) found interesting?" Arterberry asks. I'm getting better at reading his lips, but I am beginning to wonder if *he* even did the reading…. "How about (*something something*), Mr. Carlson?" he asks.

There are a number of exchanges where we get most, but not all, of the dialogue. I don't know if this is an accurate depiction of how people who lip-read experience conversation, but it made vivid for me something I hadn't thought about before. It made me imagine deafness.

Of course, it is not the job of deaf people to educate non-deaf people about what it's like to be deaf. But if this novel helps me avoid in the future the clueless behavior of some of the non-deaf characters in this novel, then I have learned a lesson that might improve accessibility in the world, if only a little. I could read in a list of rules about how important it is to face people trying to lip-read. But seeing the gaps in communication that occur when fictional characters turn away from the lip-reading narrator renders this behavior much more obvious to me than simply reading textbook suggestions. In another passage, Will also comments on an annoying and unnecessary overcompensation his teacher makes:

> Arterberry announces that "we (*something something*) very special visitors today." He starts sending people one by one down to Principal Kroener's office.

> When my turn comes, Arterberry waves in the overly showy way he always uses to communicate with me. Note to all: being deaf doesn't usually make one blind. (125)

Apparently, there are many people like Arterberry. Seeing his behavior through Will's eyes, and experiencing some of Will's emotional reaction to it, is instructive, dramatic, and memorable.

In another scene, where there's a sign language interpreter, Will tells us directly about bad behavior that can occur: "Some people talk directly to the terp and talk around the deaf person in front of them, which is like the most annoying thing in the world" (126). But because the interpreter, Melody, is young and beautiful, Will decides to have a signed conversation with her on the side, leaving the others out of the loop for a change. While the hearing people make nervous, slightly insulting jokes about Will's and Melody's private, signed conversation, we are in on both exchanges—the public one with all participants, and the private one. After one more ignorant comment from the principal, Melody signs to Will: "Is he always like this?" Will nods and is thrilled by this secret exchange. When the principal keeps going with his ignorant remarks:

> Melody and I simultaneously make the sign for "bastard" and crack each other up with swirling fingers. I am pretty sure no one else understands, but the men look disconcerted. Melody composes herself quickly, smoothing her crisp white blouse and resuming her "all-business" face—except for a tiny wink.

> A wink! She is flirting with me. Unbelievable! (127).

As readers, it's fun to be voyeurs to this hidden conversation going on right before the eyes of the ones excluded from it because they don't know sign language. In this scene it is the hearing world that becomes "the other," and readers identify with Will. This scene is also noteworthy because of how it disrupts one of an ablest culture's stereotypes about disability: that people with disabilities must live sexless lives. This novel doesn't hit us over the head in its countering of this myth; it just doesn't allow us to think for a minute that Will is not interested in sex or can't get a date.

In this novel it is the cool people who know sign language. In one scene Will has a hallway collision with a classmate named Purple Phimmul, knocking her to the floor. Without thinking, he signs his apology:

> "Sorry," I sign sorrily. My head is spinning so fast that I forget she has no idea what I am talking about. But then my head spins even faster when she signs something back."

> "How did you learn?" I ask.

> "Deaf uncle," she responds. (98)

Readers who may not know how to sign also get an occasional lesson on what some signs look like. Later in the same scene Purple has asked Will what it was that she has just seen him push under a door. He can't tell her, so he tells us, "I just keep making that sign for 'nothing,' two O shapes exploding into emptiness" (98).

Five Flavors

Five Flavors of Dumb, by Antony John, also addresses etiquette and respect, engaging readers in the drama of bad behavior. In early 2011 *Five Flavors of Dumb* won the Schneider award for the teen category for YA novels about disabilities. As librarian Barbara Klipper explains, The Schneider Family Book Award is for writing

> that artistically represents disability experiences. The books that are honored with this award not only have literary merit and reader appeal, but they portray characters whose disabilities are part of a full life, introducing young people to a diversity of experience in a way that is neither condescending nor didactic. (6)

Five Flavors is about a high school senior, Piper, who is deaf. The book's title comes from the name of the band she manages, "Dumb," and the "five flavors" refer to the unusual collection of people that make up the five members of the band. We find out early in the plot that Piper's parents (bad ones at first, of course—typical of parents who inhabit young adult novels), have used the money Piper's deaf grandparents left her (so that she could go to Gallaudet university) in order to buy expensive cochlear implants for Piper's little sister, Grace. As Roberta Seelinger Trites points out in her overview of other scholars of adolescent literature, "the lack of positive adult role models.... may well be what first defined the genre... (*Disturbing the Universe*, 9). Although she says this characterization of adults in YA literature has been gradually becoming more complex, we can see remnants of this "bad parent" tradition in this novel.

Sign language is also incorporated into the plot of this novel. In the first-person narrative the interspersing of signing (indicated by italics) and oral speech is interesting because of the added meaning behind signing: in the beginning, Piper's family only sign to her when it suits them. They sometimes deliberately do *not* sign, which is a way they can punish her a bit if she's arguing with them about something. In the following exchange Piper's parents are defending their decision to get cochlear implants for Grace. They think Piper's hearing aids are working fine, but we know that it is Piper's excellent lip-reading skills that help her compensate for her out-dated aids. The italicized prose is what she signs. As in *Dark Days*, we occasionally get a short visual description of the signs:

> *I'll never hear the way she does*, I signed, adding a little oomph as I smacked my chest (to indicate myself), and a lot of oomph as I flicked my hand toward Grace.

> "You know this wasn't an easy decision," sighed Mom, refusing to sign back to me. "But let's not forget, the implant works best on very young children, and with your residual hearing you wouldn't have been a good candidate. Besides, it wasn't covered by insurance back then."

> "It's not fully covered now either," said Dad, no doubt relieved that we were speaking, not signing. (14)

Not only have her parents used Piper's Gallaudet fund for Grace's implants, but Piper feels she's lost a potential soulmate in her little sister, now that Grace, the "*fixed* daughter," has joined the hearing world:

> ... if she remained deaf we'd be closer than mere sisters. As she grew up we'd sign nonstop, sharing words that few others could understand. I'd be there for her, help her, allow her to express herself in her own way, not demand that she conform to society's bias toward oral communication. I even came close to saying all this, but then I had an epiphany: My father wasn't indifferent to my deafness; he was mortified by it. (15–16)

Also as in *Dark Days*, Piper complains about a teacher inconsiderate of Piper's need to read his lips:

> Belson forgot to give us our homework assignment until the bell had already rung, so his announcement was made over the scraping of chairs and the ceaseless chattering of the supermodel wannabes. I couldn't catch what he said, so I had to wait for the room to clear before asking him to repeat everything to me privately. I wish I could say it was an unusual occurrence. (17).

Piper also provides some perspective on what it's like to use sign language around people who don't. In this scene, Piper gives the newly-popular band members some advice on actually making money from their music. Although the scene ends with them giving her a chance to be manager, things are uncomfortable at first, with Piper's brother Finn (who does know sign) interpreting —sometimes deliberately misrepresenting—some of the conversation. He just wants to get in the car and go home. The italics indicate signing:

> Here's a bizarre fact: When you stride up to a group of people and start signing in exaggerated gestures, conversation stops. It's completely counterintuitive really, since they could keep talking and it wouldn't interfere with my signing at all. But I knew they'd shut up, and I knew Finn would be embarrassed. At that moment, both situations seemed ideal.
>
> *Car. Now.*
>
> Finn didn't move, wouldn't even make eye contact.
>
> "What did she just say?" asked Josh, clearly unaware that I could understand him without an interpreter. (After sharing the same classes for the past three years, you'd think he'd have noticed.)
>
> "She didn't say anything," said Finn.
>
> That was the final straw. *Tell them they're crap*, I signed.
>
> "What did she say now?" pressed Josh.
>
> Finn looked at me like he truly hated my guts. "She says you're … not living up to your potential."
>
> I raised my eyebrows. Apparently Finn had a gift for improvising. Who knew? (19–20)

Piper is very angry in the beginning of the novel, and we can see why. She's treated like an alien when she enters the group. Her long-time classmate Josh (on whom Piper has a slight crush) addresses his comments to Finn, not Piper, and her normally loyal brother is not even translating her signing accurately.

Later on in this scene we witness more rude behavior through Piper's perspective. Another band member, Tash, is in on the discussion of whether or not Piper could manage the band and get them money for their appearances. Finn is still signing, though not accurately; Tash directs her conversation to Finn, not to Piper. And then, while Piper is trying to lip-read what Tash is saying, Tash turns away, and Piper is completely cut off from the conversation. Like Will in *Dark Days*, Piper hates it when people do that. As readers, we also come to see how rude it is to turn away from the person reading lips. Again, the italics indicate signing, in this case, Piper's:

> Tash shoved in front of Josh, the green spikes in her hair bristling. She flared her nostrils at me in an unflatteringly unfeminine way and turned to Finn, too unobservant to notice I'd been lip-reading all along.
>
> "So what—she thinks she could get us paid for everything, is that it?"
>
> *Yes. If you have any sense, you'll focus on charging for every interview and every appearance, instead of doing free performances on school grounds and getting suspended for it.*
>
> Finn swallowed hard. "She says…yes."
>
> Tash narrowed her eyes, and I'd swear her daubed-on-eyeliner cracked like one of those ancient oil paintings in museums.
>
> "Whatever. There's no way …"
>
> She turned away. I couldn't lip-read anymore, and her words became indistinct—a really obnoxious thing to do to someone who's hard of hearing. (21–22)

As in *Dark Days*, sign language in *Five Flavors* is used occasionally as a secret code, like when Piper and her brother Finn are trying to keep something from their parents. This novel does challenge conventional views of disability, and it makes out as villains those people who make nasty cracks about Piper's deafness (Josh, the bad guy in the band, and Mike, the bad guy manager of another band at the end)

Although I'm foregrounding Piper's deafness in this discussion, the story does not do so. In many ways, this novel is a typical coming-of-age story of a young woman finding her identity, becoming more confident, and finding her talents. Piper is deaf, but she is not stereotyped: she behaves like the adolescent she is. The band she manages, "Dumb," does make money. However, Piper's lack of hearing isn't what "saves the day" in the end. Her managing skills do.

There is an interesting scene, though, where Piper uses sign language as a secret code during negotiations concerning an important gig for the band. Piper brings her brother Finn, who signs, when she meets with Mike, the obnoxious manager of a well-known band. He desperately wants to book Piper's band to open for his band on the weekend, but he doesn't want to pay them much. Piper brings Finn, not because she needs him as an interpreter but because she knows that signing with him will rattle Mike and make him nervous. She gambles, correctly, that this staged performance can be used in her favor. Seeing this negotiation as a poker game, she signs to Finn in a separate conversation. Like the readers in *Dark Days*, in this novel we are also witness to two simultaneous conversations. It is the hearing person who doesn't know sign who is excluded from the other communication going on right in front of him. Piper is narrating. She and Finn are signing. Italics indicate sign language:

> I felt my heart racing, the memory of all those poker games I played with my dad suddenly fresh in my mind again. *Take a look at hotshot over there and tell me what he's got.*
>
> In less than a second, Finn glanced across the table and made his decision. I could tell he was looking for more chips. *He's flustered. Could be because he's annoyed about being here, but I think he's actually nervous. He blinks every time you sign, by the way…a real giveaway.*
>
> I wanted to hug Finn, but we needed to stay cool. *Good. Now keep signing to me.*
>
> *Sign what?*
>
> *Anything. Doesn't matter. Just keep going until he interrupts.*
>
> *How can you be sure he's going to—*
>
> "What's going on here?" shouted Mike, presumably for my benefit. "Are you going to sign the contract or not?" (265)

Piper and Finn continue to sign to each other. Mike gets more and more frustrated. He finally "pawed at my arm—so obnoxious. I just kept ignoring him" (266). This secret conversation gamble pays off, and Piper gets Mike to agree to pay her band over three times the fee he began with.

Whether this is negotiating in good faith is another issue. But as readers of this novel, we don't feel sorry for Mike because he's brutish and rude, and we admire Piper's cleverness. We are a bit awed by her and Finn's secret language; signing is depicted as a very useful skill to have. All the cool characters know sign or are learning it by the end. All the "bad" characters are confused or frustrated by sign language and its interpreters.

As Piper and the band members (the "five flavors") get to know one another, she becomes more confident in her identity, and some of them become more aware of accessibility issues:

> We huddled at a table next to a bay of windows. A month before, Tash and Kallie would have piled onto seats without a thought for me, but now they sat beside each other on one side, with me on the other, so that I could follow the conversation more easily. Such a small gesture, but it meant everything. (218)

By the end of the novel Piper has a nice moment with her mother, and her father is taking signing class with Piper's boyfriend, Ed, and Piper's baby sister Grace. Both parents come to "the show" at the end when Piper's group opens for a popular band.

So society (figuratively speaking) goes from sometimes deliberately turning their heads or not signing or not knowing how to sign, to being more mindful of Piper's lip-reading and to learning to sign themselves. Piper matures and becomes herself. She gets her hair cut really short and has it dyed pink. She gains confidence and becomes a really good manager. She finds and becomes comfortable with her identity. Late in the novel, Piper also finally stands up to Josh when he deliberately turns his head away, twice, as she's trying to lip-read. Josh speaks first in this exchange:

> "Oh sure. You're so important that—" He turned around as he continued speaking, like something had grabbed his attention. My heart sank, but I knew exactly what he was doing.
>
> "You'll have to repeat that, Josh," I said calmly as soon as he turned to face me again.
>
> "I said that—" Again he looked over his shoulder and I couldn't read his lips. (297–98)

A large group of people witness this disrespect, and Piper has to decide what to do about it. Finally she says:

> "Oh, Josh Josh Josh," I said sweetly. "You think that nobody here knows what you're doing. But you're wrong."
>
> For the first time the sheen wore off Josh's performance. He shifted his weight from one foot to the other.
>
> "Everyone knows I'm deaf, Josh. They know I'm reading your lips," I continued, even though I realized this was probably news to at least half the people there. "So stop trying to humiliate me. I'm not disabled, Josh, and trying to make out that I am just makes you look like an even bigger jerk than usual." (298)

The crowd does side with Piper in this scene, and it is a triumphant moment for an adolescent who is usually on the disrespected side of these encounters.

This novel also establishes that Piper is a sexual being, and she has a boyfriend at the end. As do the flirting scenes in *Dark Days*, this character's romance counters the ableist myth that people with disabilities are sexually undesirable or not interested in sex. Although this story is mostly about becoming more comfortable with one's self, the novel does challenge hegemonic views of disability, and it makes out as villains those people who make nasty cracks about Piper's deafness. It gives hearing readers some perspective on what it's like to be deaf, but that is not the main purpose of the novel. As Klipper says about what a quality YA novel on disability should include, this novel "shows characters whose lives are affected but not defined by their disabilities" (7).

The Cardturner

Another YA novel that addresses respect, etiquette, and the drama of rude behavior is an unusual novel about the game of bridge: *The Cardturner* (Delacorte, 2010), by Louis Sachar (of *Holes* fame). But unlike *Dark Days* and *Five Flavors*, which have first-person narrators who are deaf, the narrator in this novel is not deaf. In *The Cardturner*, the protagonist and first person narrator is a seventeen-year-old named Alton Richards, who is a cardturner for his uncle Lester Trapp, a life-long bridge player. Uncle Lester is in his seventies, diabetic, and has recently become blind because of the diabetes. He plays bridge by memorizing the cards, which other players describe out loud to him as the game progresses. Alton turns the cards his uncle tells him to and says what they are. The uncle's blindness is treated as neither pitiable nor heroic, though he becomes almost heroic in his nephew's eyes because he is such a good bridge player. Most people who know Mr. Trapp well treat him like everyone else.

There are some moments, however, where foolish, sometimes mean people who inhabit the "normal" world behave in a way that disrespects Alton's uncle because of his blindness. We don't get Mr. Trapp's thoughts on these moments, and we're not asked to identify with him. He's aloof, almost gruff towards Alton, and he rarely says anything about these behaviors. We experience these moments of disrespect through the narrator's eyes, whose view of his uncle changes as he gets to know him.

One of these moments of disrespect occurs when Alton and Mr. Trapp go to a tournament, which is held in a location other than Mr. Trapp's usual bridge club, where he knows and is respected by everyone. When they walk across this new room to get settled at their table, they pass people who don't know them:

> People stopped and stared at us as we made our way to our assigned table.

> "Can't be worse than the partner I had this morning," I heard someone say with a laugh.

> *Just you wait*, I thought. *We're going to kick your ass!* (126)

Alton, who began by being merely curious about this relative he barely knew (he refers to him neutrally as "Trapp" throughout the novel), has come to respect him. Being a teenager, Alton is acutely attuned to what people think and to the comments muttered as they walk through the room. He picks up on the disrespect immediately and reacts to it in his head.

In the following scene, we see other behavior clearly depicted as rude. A bridge game has just started at this tournament, where strangers play cards together, and where the first and only thing people know about Mr. Trapp is that he is blind. Unlike the people in his bridge club at home, these people are unfamiliar with the process of Alton's cardturning. They address their remarks to Alton, not his uncle. ("East" and "West" are names Alton uses to refer to the positions these two people play in the bridge game.)

The game got under way. I removed the South hand from board seventeen, then led Trapp to a nearby corner.

"So, you just told him all his cards?" East asked when we returned.

"And he's going to remember them?" asked West.

"You can ask me," my uncle said. "Despite my lack of eyesight, I can hear and speak."

As readers, we see through Alton's eyes that the two new bridge partners, East and West, are rude or at best ignorant in directing their questions to Alton, not to Mr. Trapp, who is right there in front of them. The scene continues with Gloria, Mr. Trapp's longtime bridge partner, playing the "pass" card and also saying it out loud for the benefit of her blind partner. This slight change in routine throws the two new players for a loop:

"Pass," said Gloria as she set a green pass card on the table.

"Are we supposed to say our bids out loud?" asked East.

"It would be helpful," said Trapp.

"One heart," she said, but then set the 1 [of spades] card on the table.

Gloria pointed out the discrepancy, and the woman apologized, complaining about how confusing it was to have to say a bid out loud when using bidding boxes.

Here we see human pettiness or stupidity through Alton's eyes, whose own perspective on his uncle's disability has only recently changed. In a later scene at that same tournament, East and West think Mr. Trapp is somehow cheating because of his blindness and because of Alton's presence:

West admonished her partner to hold her hand back.

"He can't *see* my cards!" East exclaimed.

"The kid can see," said West. "There's something funny going on between them."

"Now, hold on!" warned Gloria.

The situation intensifies until the director must be called over—the equiv-alent, in bridge, of calling the authorities to sort out a dispute. Penalties are given out, but then the director tells the two sets of partners to continue the game:

> The director told us to go on to the next hand and advised everyone to treat the other players with respect. "This is a zero-tolerance tournament."

> "Well, it's very distracting when we have to keep saying every card out loud," complained East.

> "I'm sorry my partner's blindness makes life so difficult for you," said Gloria.

The chapter ends with that comment. There are other scenes where the novel is clearly constructed in a way that will make us disapprove of these mean, foolish people and their ableist attitudes and behaviors.

Discussing These Novels

The discussions that take place before or after reading any one of these three novels are critical in making sure the rudeness of some of the characters is seen as such by readers. Stereotypes, even when they are disapproved in the novel itself, can be misread by some readers who might hold those stereotypes themselves and simply read right over the bad behavior, not seeing that readers are supposed to disapprove of it. Discussion questions, therefore, must be framed so readers can learn from these scenes, and comments students make in class must be listened to and responded to carefully.

On the web are a variety of questions posted by teachers and/or students using *Five Flavors* in schools or book clubs. Some ask readers to "predict" what will happen next in the plot, an approach many believe stimulates reading comprehension skills. Some are simple right or wrong recall questions, such as "What school did Piper want to go to?" There is nothing inherently wrong with such low-level questions, other than that they can be mind-numbingly boring and take time away from what might be a more challenging and interesting use of time. Depending on the teacher's or discussion leader's articulated or unarticulated assumptions concerning the purpose(s) of reading this or any text, the questions, if considered carefully, should reflect those assumptions about purpose. And maybe the purpose for some questions begins and ends at reading comprehension and fact recall. Unless the questions are deliberately posed in a way that will draw attention to the text as a representation of ableist or counter-hegemonic views, it's unlikely that the typical web-available question will ask readers to consider the text from this perspective.

Different questions would stimulate more sophisticated discussions and more interaction with the text. For example, one question to ask about *Five Flavors* might be, "What do you think of Piper's parents' decision regarding her sister's cochlear implants?" This question might spark a follow-up project that involves research on Gallaudet University, cochlear implants, and some of the ongoing debates about their use. For *Dark Days*, students might be asked, "When Will glanced at the principal's paperwork, he saw himself described as 'profoundly deaf yet intellectually capable.'" Why does this phrase upset him so much? What does the word *yet* imply? How would that phrase be different if *and* were substituted for *yet?*" For the Sachar novel, students might be asked this question: "In *The Cardturner*, Mr. Trapp's bridge partner, Gloria, says to the other people they're playing with that day, 'I'm sorry my partner's blindness makes life so difficult for you.' In what tone of voice do you think Gloria would deliver that line? What makes you say so?" Such questions also promote better reading comprehension and gathering of evidence from the text, tasks many teachers are rightly concerned with. But these questions might also get readers with or without disabilities to imagine a world with fewer constructed obstacles.

In addition to questions specific to one novel, there are open-ended questions that might allow students to think further about issues in all three novels covered in this chapter: "What do you think of the way some of the main character's family members and friends treat her or him?" "Why do some characters change the way they interact with the main character?" Some questions from the editors' introduction to *Disability and the Teaching of Writing* might also be adapted to these and other YA novels about disability:

> What attitudes about disability and disabled people shape perceptions and actions by students and teachers?

> What social, physical, and learning barriers complicate access to learning for disabled students and to teaching for disabled teachers?

> What literacy skills are developed when embodied differences and disability are included as topics in the curriculum? (Lewieki-Wilson, Brueggemann, with Dolmage, 2)

In *Five Flavors*, *Dark Days*, and *The Cardturner*, there are characters who display attitudes about disability that could be discussed. All three characters with disabilities in those respective novels encounter barriers—both physical and social—that were constructed by society and could be removed by society, if it has the will to do so. The question about literacy skills is also relevant to all three novels because, in each story, there are what would be considered new or unusual communication strategies used by some of the main characters, strategies they've developed because of their particular impairment.

It's not that discussions of these novels need to focus exclusively on disability or on society's fraught relationship with it. Readers can still be asked about vocabulary, plot points, literary figures, and the rest. The point is that these texts offer a rich opportunity for critical engagement with both the text and the society that produced it. A few well-placed questions can stimulate that critical engagement.

· 3 ·

AWAKENING STORIES:
"THE SCARLET IBIS" AND *THE CAY*

In this chapter I discuss two pieces of older fiction which were both written
in the mid-20th century, won prizes, and are still read widely in schools today:
"The Scarlet Ibis," an anthologized short story by James Hurst, and *The Cay*,
a short children's novel by Theodore Taylor. "The Scarlet Ibis" is often taught
in ninth grade and *The Cay* usually in fifth or other middle grades. While not
in a strict category of "young adult" that requires texts be written specifically
for young adults or teens, these pieces are both stories in which the adult
narrator has an epiphany regarding something from his childhood. He comes
to regret the way he treated someone else when he was a boy. Both pieces
have a character with an impairment. In "The Scarlet Ibis" that character is
the narrator's brother, referred to as "an invalid" who was born "with a tiny
body which was red and shriveled like an old man's." In *The Cay*, the narrator
becomes blind when he's hit on the head by a timber during a ship wreck but
then is cured at the end of the story. To my knowledge, neither author had a
disability.

Regarding these two canonical pieces, it's important to analyze the
reception documents that shape classroom discussion as well as the texts
themselves. To what extent do these texts and their accompanying classroom
activities challenge or cement "disabled" and "nondisabled" as always separate

categories? Because these texts have been used in the schools for decades, they have spawned all manner of summaries, reviews, analyses, discussion questions, quizzes, and entries on social media widely available through a quick web search. I will also examine selections of these reception materials because they can help us understand how these two texts have been received and for what purposes they seem to be used.

"The Scarlet Ibis" was first published in *The Atlantic Monthly* in 1960 but set in 1918. It is a retrospective, told in the first person by an adult relating events that occurred in his childhood. When it was published, it won the Atlantic First award and has been included in different publishers' literature anthologies for decades. It is a fictional piece about a narrator who, at age six, was disappointed when his younger brother was born small and weak from a heart condition. The baby's name is William Armstrong, but the narrator (referred to as "Brother") and the family call him Doodle because of the "doodle bug" manner in which he makes his way across the floor. Because the father expected the baby to die, he had built for him "a little mahogany coffin." The narrator considers "smothering him with a pillow" but changes his mind when the baby smiles at him, though he considers him "a burden" because his mother always made him take his younger brother with him.

The narrator is ashamed that his brother can't walk, so as both boys grow older he pushes Doodle to his physical limits until he can take some steps. Thrilled at this progress, the brother pushes Doodle even harder, forcing him to climb rope vines, "swim until he turned blue, and row until he couldn't lift an oar." One day, during a storm, the brother runs away from Doodle, even though Doodle begs him not to leave him. When the narrator finally feels guilty enough to return, Doodle is dead, collapsed in a position similar to a dead scarlet ibis that had appeared in the yard earlier after a similar storm. He is also "bleeding from the mouth, and his neck and the front of his shirt were stained a brilliant red." The younger boy's death provides a lesson for his brother, who realizes that he has been too proud and cruel in his efforts to make Doodle "normal." The story, therefore, is an epiphany for the older brother, and the character with the impairment must die so that the narrator can have this enlightenment or awakening. "The Scarlet Ibis" is about the older brother, not Doodle. However, what ideas about disability do children absorb when stories like this are read and discussed for generations in the schools, especially when the discussions, as we will see, focus mostly on generic themes and obvious symbols? Doodle's death at the end serves as a lesson for the narrator. How often are students asked how stories such as this, and endings such as this, position characters with impairments? What lessons do stories like this one teach readers about disability?

The Cay, published in 1969 and dedicated to Dr. Martin Luther King's dream, is a short (105 page) children's novel—a bestseller, with over four million copies sold (Bernstein). Set in 1942, it is also a retrospective told by an adult of an adventure he had as a child, in this case when he was eleven. After a vessel on which he was traveling was attacked in World War II by a German submarine, narrator Phillip finds himself on a raft with an older West Indian man named Timothy, and a cat. A bump Phillip received on his head during the escape from the sinking ship soon causes him to go blind, after which he becomes almost totally dependent on Timothy. They manage to reach land, an uninhabited cay. Phillip survives by using his other senses and Timothy's ingenious strategies for helping Phillip navigate the small island, even after Timothy dies after sheltering the boy during a fierce storm. Phillip is eventually seen and rescued. In this novel the narrator functions as both a non-disabled and a disabled character, being sighted, then blind, then sighted again in the space of 105 pages. At the end of *The Cay*, in a short paragraph, we're told that Phillip's blindness is cured:

> Four months later, in a hospital in New York, after many X rays and tests, I had the first of three operations. The piece of timber that had hit me the night the *Hato* went down had damaged some nerves. But after the third operation, when the bandages came off, I could see again. I would always have to wear glasses, but I could see. That was the important thing." (Taylor 104)

The boy-on-a-raft part of this fictional story was inspired by a real event that happened in World War II. Taylor read about a German submarine that torpedoed a Dutch ship and a young boy who managed to get to a raft, but drifted off into the sea when the people trying to rescue him lost him in the darkness (Sieruta). In what seems to be a misogynist trend in fiction, Phillip's mother is characterized as a closed-minded worrier and racist. His father, however, is characterized as wise and noble. As we will see in other YA novels discussed in this book, negative characterizations of mothers are fairly common, while fathers are typically portrayed as merely bumbling.[1]

The Cay received numerous awards, including the Jane Addams Children's Book Award in 1970, but several years later, because of objections by the Council on Interracial Books for Children, the prize was rescinded. According to Sieruta, an article by Albert V. Schwartz that appeared in the Council's journal criticized *The Cay* for what Schwartz saw as the "subservient" portrayal of Timothy and the cementing of white values. The book was also criticized for its use of dialect (Sieruta). (For a long time, Timothy calls Phillip "young bahss," until, about halfway through the book, when, after a racist rant on Phillip's part and an angry reaction from Timothy, they make up, and the boy asks Timothy to call him Phillip (55).[2] In spite of the controversy that surrounded its treatment of racial issues and being banned in some school libraries, *The Cay* is still widely read today, probably because it is a short, fast-moving adventure about a ship wreck and a desert island and has lots of sensory imagery. It also has a painfully obvious metaphor about a racist child's "blindness" about race.

Reinforcing Disability Myths

Here's a problem with these two canonical texts: in one story, the child with the disability dies in the end; in the other, the child's blindness is cured almost miraculously in the last pages. In "The Scarlet Ibis" and *The Cay*, what happens to the character with the impairment strongly reinforces several of the disability myths (discussed further in Chapter Five) that Jay Dolmage, and others he credits, have outlined. In one Interchapter of his book *Disability Rhetoric*, "An Archive and Anatomy of Disability Myths," Jay Dolmage describes one of these myths as "Kill-or-Cure":

> Just as a loaded gun shown in the opening scenes of a movie will eventually be fired, a disabled character will either have to be "killed or cured" by the end of any movie or novel in which they appear. This death or cure will often seem to "redeem" the protagonist—the death will be sacrificial, or the cure will be credited to the hero. (39)

In "The Scarlet Ibis," Doodle's is the sacrificial death that "redeems" the narrator. He comes to regret the way he treated his brother, and he learns that pride is a bad thing. In *The Cay*, the restoration of the narrator's sight symbolizes his redemption from the "blindness" of racial prejudice. Bev Brenna, in her analysis of several Canadian children's novels, also draws on patterns numerous scholars have observed regarding characters with disabilities. She summarizes Lois Keith's enumeration of these patterns, one of which is that "the impairment is curable" (Brenna 3). If in one of the few texts in the school curriculum about disability the impairment is magically gone by the end, students may develop unrealistic expectations about cure. They may also internalize the idea that it is impossible to live a fulfilled life with a disability.

In each of these pieces of fiction the unspoken message about disability is that it has no place in society. For decades, students have been reading, discussing, analyzing, and taking quizzes on these two texts. Together or alone, these texts have a disturbing message. Students who read one or both of them, but few other texts written by real people with impairments (or other texts with more positive and/or realistic representations of disability), may absorb the unspoken message that people with impairments should either get better or die. Because this message is implied but not stated, it remains unnamed, undiscussed, and unchallenged, unless the teacher poses questions or problems about the implications of these endings. The possibility that a character could live, let alone live happily, with the particular impairment is not pursued.

An online exploration of reception documents provides some insight into how these texts are talked about in the schools. For both texts, there are many such documents available. What follows is a representative sample. In each case, most discussion questions focus on the usual suspects in a high school literature class: vocabulary, theme, sensory imagery, symbolism and metaphor, and these two texts are replete with opportunities to bombard students, once again, with these simple New Critical aspects of literature.

Reception Documents for "The Scarlet Ibis"

"The Scarlet Ibis" is the perfect story for those whose main purpose in having students read texts is to point to "literary elements." The symbol is so obvious in this piece that it appears as the title and also in the last two words of the story. Should sleepy readers possibly fail to see it, most materials designed for class discussions or quizzes on this short story focus relentlessly on symbolism and the similarities between Doodle and the scarlet ibis.

There are some exceptions to this pattern. Tanya Merritt, in a hard-to-find critique of "The Scarlet Ibis" which appears in an *English Journal* article, questions the attitude Doodle's family has toward him: "When I read 'The Scarlet Ibis,' I always feel sorrow for Doodle's mother because we never see her loving Doodle for who he is and what he can do. For whatever reason, both parents appear to define Doodle by his limitations" (54). In addition, the popular website Shmoop.com, a resource for students looking for background and interpretations of texts commonly used in the schools, has some thought-provoking questions about "The Scarlet Ibis":

Here, an older brother is coaching his younger brother, who has physical disabilities, on how to fit in while in school. This story raises all sorts of important questions: Why is it that we sometimes fear people who are different? Why do many people think it's so important to fit in? If someone doesn't mind being different, why do we often still pressure them to conform? This story shows that pushing others *too* hard to fit in can end in tragedy. (Shmoop)

Shmoop also critiques the way Doodle was treated by the medical establishment in 1911: "If he'd had a little help from a perceptive doctor, willing to compromise, he might have been able to understand that Doodle was fragile, and did need special care, but that he could still lead an active physical life." This is a rare comment that suggests the possibility of a good life for Doodle, though there are no questions asking students to think about the implications of having a character like Doodle die at the end in order to provide a moral epiphany for his non-disabled brother.

One blogger, in what appears to be a student's response to "The Scarlet Ibis," does write that "One of the author's main points is that people should not change anyone so they are more appealing to a particular person or to society." This is an insightful conclusion to draw from this story. Unfortunately, this blogger describes Doodle as "physically and mentally handicapped" (Heiser). It's possible that she missed the scene in which Doodle's family concludes that he is, indeed, "all there." It's also possible that she's conflating physical and mental disabilities, which, of course, Doodle's family does early on, too.

Much more common, however, are reception materials such as the following, which make it seem like the only reason one would ever read fiction is to locate the symbol. One example is the Wikipedia entry on "The Scarlet Ibis." Under the heading of "Analysis," there are only three sentences; they mention symbolism, the scarlet ibis, and the color red ("The Scarlet Ibis" Wikipedia). Also typical are some questions about literary devices and symbolism, versions of which appear in numerous sites on the web (only one is referenced here): "How is Doodle's death similar to the birds' [sic] death? Explain in detail." And, of course, there is the inevitable question about "literary devices": "What literary devices does Hurst use to tell his story? How do these devices help make the story effective? Offer textual support from the text" ("The Scarlet Ibis" Wikispaces.com).

A similar reception document is a webquest in which the main purpose is to "define and identify a symbol" (Selwochi and Dunn). Another such resource for this story is a document at the website CurriculumCompanion.org, associated with anthology publishers. It begins with vocabulary, theme, predictions, inferences, etc. As do most of these resources, there is a question on Literary Analysis. This slide has two bullet points: "It is important to recognize and interpret an important symbol." The second one: "In what ways is the bird like doodle?" [sic] ("Ninth Grade Resources"). Many lesson plans ask students for "specific evidence from the text" to support their thesis that the scarlet ibis is a symbol for Doodle.

After the many days of vocabulary definitions, symbol hunts, and "textual evidence" listings for "literary analysis" essays in unit plans like these, what lessons do students learn about society and people with impairments? And how will they unlearn them?

Reception Documents for *The Cay*

Similarly, most reception documents for *The Cay* focus on the adventure, the fast-moving plot, and Phillip's prejudice. Phillip's blindness in *The Cay*, as most reception documents emphasize, is more than a physical blindness. It is, of course, a metaphor for his racist blindness regarding Timothy. Not much is said about his physical blindness, which sets in several days after he's hit on the head by a ship timber as he escapes the sinking ship, except as how the blindness functions as a metaphor.

In one insightful summary, however, the website Shmoop.com refreshingly calls Phillip's blindness a "handy metaphor for his changing world view before he is miraculously cured at the end of the novel." Shmoop is one of the rare online resources that has a somewhat cynical attitude toward the plot, and poses an unusual question about *The Cay*. They ask, "What would have happened if Phillip hadn't been saved by an operation? " (Shmoop Editorial Team, 2008). In its separate webpage of questions on *The Cay*, however, Shmoop lists more conventional questions about war, violence, friendship, and what the tempest might symbolize. (Shmoop Editorial Team). There are no questions about what role Phillip's *deus ex machina* cure might play in reinscribing disability myths.

The commercial publishers of this novel, or in whose anthologies "The Scarlet Ibis" appears, frequently have online resources for teachers and ready-made quizzes for students. The Random House "Teachers Guide," [sic] written by Pat Scales, summarizes the plot of *The Cay* and lists some vocabulary words as well as the awards the book received (six, not including the one that was given and taken away), as well as a number of themes, among them survival, courage, and racial prejudice. There are some suggested cross-curricular activities, among them having students research Dr. Martin Luther King's dream, calypso music, steel drums, geography of the area of the cay, and voodoo (Scales). There is nothing that questions the almost magical restoration of Phillip's eyesight at the end, or what the implications of that cure might be for real people who are blind.

In "A Study Guide" on *The Cay*, designed by Marcia Tretler, eight out of ten Anticipation Questions on the novel address prejudice, but focus on "ethnic or religious" issues, not disability (Tretler). Finally, there are a number of websites that align these texts with the Common Core State Standards, the juggernaut plowing through most public schools in the second decade of this century. There are also sites addressing "text complexity," an overwrought issue on average word and sentence length that in too many schools has overwhelmed possibilities of critical thinking about disability.

Critical Questions We Might Pose

I have yet to find critical questions on the web that address what message these representations of disability (death or cure) might give to young readers about the lived experiences of real people with impairments (though I'll keep looking). Here are some questions that might be used to launch more critical discussions of disability and to what extent these or other texts challenge, complicate, reflect, or reinforce societal assumptions about disability:

- What happens to the character with the disability at the end?
- What do you think of that ending?
- What message does it seem to deliver, in an unspoken way, about disability?
- What do you think of that message?
- Besides the bodily weakness William Armstrong (Doodle) was born with in "The Scarlet Ibis," what other factors contributed most to his disability? What might his life had been like had he been born into a different family, a different society?
- At the end of *The Cay*, Phillip says, after his operation, "…when the bandages came off, I could see again. I would always have to wear glasses, but I could see. That was the important thing" (104). What messages might this ending give to readers about blindness?

Teachers can and will, continue to ask questions about plot, imagery, and, of course, the "literary elements" and on-the-nose symbols in these texts. But teachers can enrich the discussion and possibly mitigate some of the binarizing abled/disabled effects of these stories by also posing critical questions about the role these texts play in contributing to disability myths.

As Kathy Saunders argues in her *Disability Studies Quarterly* article on Disability Studies and children's literature:

> The insight that disability scholars can bring to analysis of children's literature lies in their understanding of "disability" not as a personalized, wholly biological and medically mediated characteristic, but as a social construction evidenced in texts as the described attitudes of both disabled and non-disabled characters, and in the rationale of plots which both create and consolidate the attitudes and circumstances that are commonly found in contemporary society." (Saunders)

Middle schoolers are capable of understanding the ideas in this passage, if not the vocabulary and syntax. It is up to responsible teachers to translate what Saunders writes about here and bring it into class discussions of "The Scarlet Ibis," *The Cay*, and other texts read for their display of literary devices but which also carry with them implicit yet powerful messages and myths about disability.

In her section of a larger piece in *Disability Studies Quarterly* called "Questioning Representations of Disability in Adolescent Literature," Valerie Struthers Walker includes some questions general enough to be useful in discussions of either piece discussed in this chapter. One excellent question she poses is, "How do our own experiences and beliefs shape the meanings we make of representations of disability in texts?" (Walker, Mileski, Greaves, & Patterson). Tara Mileski's question about Choldenko's YA novel, *Al Capone Does My Shirts* (another novel where a non-disabled character narrates a story about a disabled sibling), is also useful for "The Scarlet Ibis" and *The Cay*: "How would the story be different if it were set in a contemporary period? Does reading this book as historical fiction make you think about this type of labeling as a thing of the past? Or is it still a problem?" (Walker, Mileski, Greaves, & Patterson).

"Enlightenment Narratives"

One useful concept in posing questions about these two stories is the "enlightenment" or "conversion narrative," explained by Amy Vidali, Margaret Price, and Cynthia Lewiecki-Wilson, who show how this concept can be problematic. In the Introduction to their special issue of *Disability Studies Quarterly* on "Disability Studies in the Undergraduate Classroom," these scholars explain how this problem sometimes manifests in reflections college students write after having read texts about disability. If students read stories about disability for the first time, they often talk about how much they have learned; they become "enlightened" or "converted" to a new way of thinking about disability. As described by Vidali, Price, and Lewiecki-Wilson, in the "enlightenment narratives" the disability functions as an "educational device." They warn that reflections about reading or learning about disability often "invite a familiar enlightenment narrative, along the lines of "now that I have read about/seen/ spoken to (a) disabled person(s), my mind has been opened." This enlightenment narrative reifies assumptions about "disabled" and "nondisabled" as rigid categories and implies that disabled persons exist in order to serve as educational devices" (Vidali, Price, and Lewiecki-Wilson). To a certain extent, "The Scarlet Ibis" and *The Cay* may function as "enlightenment narratives." "The Scarlet Ibis," for example, evokes sympathy for Doodle and shame on the part of the narrator for his entreaties to his brother to "try harder." In fact, the questioning of the entreaty to disabled people to simply "try harder" to overcome their impairment (a topic discussed more thoroughly in Chapter Four), may in fact be one of the more useful discussion points engendered by this short story. However, it is Doodle's death that enlightens the narrator to his own selfishness and pride.

For some readers, *The Cay* may also function as a limited "enlightenment narrative" because there is some non-visual sensory imagery as Phillip learns to navigate the island without his sight. Some descriptions show him using his other senses, as well as what he learned from Timothy, to survive until he is finally rescued. When an airplane approaches and Timothy tries to get the pilot's attention with flame, Phillip tells us, "The faint drone of the aircraft seemed closer now. In a moment, I smelled cloth burning and knew he was holding the wrapped piece of wood toward the sky" (36). He describes the rain and wind: "It peppered in bursts against the frond roof, and I could hear the drips as it leaked through. The squall wind was in the tops of the palms, and I could imagine how they looked in the night sky, thrashing against each other over our little cay" (56–57). Although these descriptions might provide some enlightenment for readers regarding how blind people can access their other senses, the novel is really not about a successful blind person but rather about how Phillip's moral blindness is cured. Once this boy who is "blinded" by his prejudice and racism learns to "see" the humanity of the man with whom he is shipwrecked, he gains his physical sight back as well.

"Narrative Prosthesis"

In each of these two narratives, the disability functions mostly as a metaphor. As is repeatedly stressed in lesson plans on "The Scarlet Ibis," the exotic bird is a symbol of Doodle. Both die in storms. The bird is red. Doodle has some red blood trickling from his mouth when his brother finds him dead. In *The Cay*, Phillip's temporary blindness is a metaphor for his moral blindness and prejudice concerning race. In each case, the disability is a plot device, not a serious consideration of realistic views of disability in society. Both of these stories fit into a pattern similar to what Mitchell and Snyder describe as a "narrative prosthesis":

> Our thesis centers not simply upon the fact that people with disabilities have been the object of representational treatments, but rather that their function in literary discourse is primarily twofold: disability pervades literary narrative, first, as a stock feature of characterization and, second, as an opportunistic metaphorical device. We term this perpetual discursive dependence upon disability *narrative prosthesis*. (47)

After, say, a week-long lesson plan on the vocabulary, themes, and symbols in texts like these, students might come away from class discussions with the notion that people with disabilities just simply die, get cured, and/or function simply as metaphors. To counter that myth, teachers should also pose other questions about such literature.

Middle school children are capable of stepping back from a text and discussing the overall effect a novel and its depictions of characters and/or situations might have on readers. Teachers might, for example, ask, "How realistic is it that someone's total blindness can be fixed so easily? What might readers infer from this scene about an almost miraculous cure for blindness—about people whose blindness is not cured by a few operations?" They might also briefly explain Mitchell and Snyder's concept of "narrative prosthesis" in language children can understand and then ask questions about how these stories, or other stories in the canon, illustrate that theory in practice.

"Awakening Stories"

Another concept useful in analyzing literature is Jacqueline Jones Royster's concept of "white man's awakening stories," that is, stories that seem aimed at naïve or uneducated readers who do not know what other groups already know because of their lived experience. These stories have the potential to help some groups think about issues they have never thought about before (Royster). In a keynote speech she delivered to the Rhetoric Society of America in 1998, Royster explained this concept, which is worth some explanation here.

Royster's concept was part of her brilliant analysis of the 1997 film *Amistad*, about a ship involved in kidnapping and enslaving Africans.[3] Although the film was based on the true story of the successful revolt led by Senghe Pieh, one of the kidnapped Africans, Royster points out that the film "made central the white men in the story" (42). It became what she calls "a white man's awakening story," through which the "filmmakers situate the participants in the discourse as performers and viewers in a way that permits concerns to become visible and thereby capable of being discussed" (41). She argues that the story of the revolt and of the subsequent trial provided "the opportunity to make visible the previously invisible—in white men's eyes, of course" (42).[4] Royster's concept of the "awakening story," as she shows how it functions regarding sensitive issues regarding slavery and race, is a useful concept to theorize how some stories of disability function. In *Amistad*, the spotlight is on the white lawyer, Robert Baldwin, played by Matthew McConaughhey, and on the character of John Quincy Adams, played by Sir Anthony Hopkins. The protagonist is not the heroic defendant who had led the revolt. The story, Royster argues, is framed as the awakening story for McConaughhey's character, who comes to see the hero of the revolt as a man, as "human." This awakening story tactic, "permits concerns to become visible and otherwise capable of being discussed" (41).

Similarly, *The Cay* functions as an "awakening story" about race for Phillip, the white, non-disabled, then blinded, then non-disabled-again, narrator, who develops a somewhat more mature and sophisticated view of people and of the world. The novel may also function that way for some readers, or may have functioned that way in 1969, when the book was published. Although Phillip does have a new appreciation of his other senses and learns to use them to survive on the island, this novel is mostly about a young white boy learning that Timothy, the older West Indian man, can be a generous, smart human being. Phillip's epiphany is about race, not disability. In that sense, the novel fits well into Royster's "white man's awakening story" (42) model. Perhaps *The Cay* is (or was) an awakening story about race for some readers as well, though many readers object to its representation of Timothy and its unchallenged reinforcement of Phillip's values and judgments. Similarly, this novel's unspoken message about disability is a behind-the-scenes reinforcement of a harmful myth in society.

Ironically, as Royster went on to point out in her analysis of *Amistad*, the issues of race and slavery in that film were not, in the end, discussed much at the time: "… the film was actually unable to generate such a discussion. *Amistad* was neither widely seen nor widely discussed, …" (42). As we have seen, there is a similar pattern of silence regarding Phillip's physical blindness in *The Cay*. After reading this novel, students are asked to discuss prejudice, and the controversy about Timothy's portrayal also started some discussion about race. However, as the reception documents available on the web today seem to indicate, there is not much questioning about how disability is represented in *The Cay*, let alone whether that representation disrupts, or cements, harmful notions about disability.

"The Scarlet Ibis" also reinforces a disability myth. In the end, Doodle dies, suggesting that life with his impairment is intolerable. The adult narrator does come to regret his insistent, childish advice to Doodle that "All you got to do is try" [to learn to walk]. Doodle's character, therefore, functions mainly as a tool to show the growth and regret of the non-disabled narrator as he looks back at his childhood. Doodle dies at the end, one more disabled character who becomes a sacrifice at the altar of the narrator's moral growth.

Using disabled characters as tools or reflections of moral growth is not unusual. In his analysis of Faulkner's *The Sound and the Fury*, Michael Bérubé argues that this novel "positions Benji as the moral arbiter of the rest of the characters, who are measured by the standard of how they treat the least of the Compson brothers" (575). In other words, the disabled character, especially the way his siblings characters treat him, is used as a way to characterize those others. In "The Scarlet Ibis," Doodle is used in a similar way. The dead bird in the story, the scarlet ibis, is a painfully obvious symbol for the dead child. It would be difficult for those whose primary objective is to teach symbolism to find a better story. And if there is any ninth grader in the world who manages to read this story and not trip over the similarities between the scarlet ibis and Doodle, there are dozens of study guides and questions on the web to make sure that reader can explain that almighty literary device, with a parade of "textual evidence."

If these widely read, canonical texts are students' primary exposure to characters with impairments, there are several dangerous messages about disability that students receive. From "The Scarlet Ibis" they learn that Doodle is mostly used as a gauge of the narrator's moral development, and that people like him die young. From *The Cay* they learn that blindness must be cured. Although the novel does provide some vivid non-visual sensory imagery, and Phillip does learn to survive by himself by sound, touch, taste, and smell, blindness is still represented as an impairment that cannot be tolerated. As Pamela S. Carroll and L. Penny Rosenblum point out: "This back-to-normal theme may communicate to adolescents with visual impairments that a story can have a happy ending only when the blindness is removed. It may also give adolescents and their peers a false hope that blindness or low vision will be cured" (625). When using these texts, we need to challenge these dangerous messages by pointing them out if necessary or posing questions designed to help students see them for themselves.

These two canonical texts, together with the teaching materials that accompany them, occasionally challenge, but mostly reinforce, ableist binaries regarding disability. These texts, therefore, and the reception documents that accompanying them, may be doing a lot more than providing opportunities for the teaching of symbols and sensory imagery. They may be quietly reinforcing harmful societal assumptions about disability. To counter that effect, teachers need to add to the plot/theme/symbol questions typically found on the web. Better yet, we can add novels, short stories, poetry, and non-fiction written by people with disabilities that provide a counter-narrative to these "classics."

Notes

1. See, for example, discussions in Chapter Five on *From Charlie's Point of View* and *The Dark Days of Hamburger Halpin*. Also see Chapter Four for a discussion of how *Peeling the Onion* and especially *The Absolutely True Diary of a Part-Time Indian* present strong counter-narratives to those negative representations of older women.

2. A modified version of *The Cay* is used in some schools. However, it is the depiction of Timothy that is considered controversial, not the almost magical "cure" of Phillip's blindness and that ending's implications for reinforcing disability myths.

3. I am grateful to Ken Lindblom for reminding me about Dr. Royster's speech and how it might apply to this topic.

4. Royster's keynote speech was later published: Royster, Jacqueline J. "Sarah's Story: Making a Place for Historical Ethnography in Rhetorical Studies." In *Rhetoric, the Polis, and the Global Village: Proceedings from the 1998 Rhetoric Society of America Conference*. Edited by C. Jan Swearingen and Dave Pruett. Mahwah, NJ: Lawrence Erlbaum Associates, 1999: 39–51.

· 4 ·

CARVING OUT AN IDENTITY: *PEELING THE ONION, STONER AND SPAZ,* AND *THE ABSOLUTELY TRUE DIARY OF A PART-TIME INDIAN*

It is not unusual for YA protagonists to carve out new identities throughout the course of their narratives. As Sherman Alexie puts it, "Literature is all about the search for identity, regardless of the ethnicity" (Chapel). Young protagonists often have conflicts with themselves, their parents or siblings, their friends, their teachers, their sports teams, or their communities. An added dimension to the novels discussed in this chapter is that these narrators, all of whom have a significant physical impairment, learn something else in the process: over the course of their development, they learn to question society's apparent assumptions about disability, which they have unconsciously applied to themselves. In fact, to varying degrees, finding their new identity is directly tied to changing a number of views society has taught them to hold, about disability, and about groups unlike themselves. In this chapter, I will be examining Wendy Orr's *Peeling the Onion,* juxtaposing it throughout to Ron Koertge's *Stoner and Spaz,* and to Sherman Alexie's *The Absolutely True Diary of a Part-Time Indian,* tracing the three protagonists' growth toward identity and simultaneous movement away from various prejudices these characters had absorbed about themselves or others.

In two cases, the narrators' societies become more welcoming; and in one case, society's less welcoming aspects become more visible to the narrator, who learns to reject some of its dictates. This chapter will also explore the extent to which each text is doing "cultural work," Jane Tompkins' phrase for questioning a text's impact on changing the world. Texts can challenge society's views of certain groups, cement existing views, or even construct more negative views. A text's artistic value notwithstanding, we must question its impact and reception. Does it complicate or reinforce cultural stereotypes? Does it make society more inclusive or less accessible? In short, does the text make the world better or worse? As Alexie has said about his writing:

> 'I've come to the realization that many people have been reading literary fiction for the same reason they read mainstream fiction,' he says. 'For entertainment and a form of escape. I don't want to write books that provide people with that. I want books that challenge, anger, and possibly offend.' (Cline 197).

Judging by the challenges *True Diary* has received, Alexie has achieved that goal, and as we will see, the other two books in this chapter have also challenged or angered some readers. *Peeling the Onion* has received mixed reviews, as have *True Diary* and *Stoner and Spaz*, but for different reasons. Every year, some parents want *True Diary* banned because of its talk of "boners" or its racist joke, even though that comment is meant to characterize both the teller of the joke and narrator Arnold, who punches him. Alexie has also been criticized for his depiction of alcoholism and despair on the reservation (McNally 28). Some reviewers warn parents against *Stoner and Spaz*, too, mostly because of one character's drug use, even though the story makes it clear that drugs are very bad and will no doubt kill her one day. Similarly, adults' objections to *Stoner and Spaz* mostly center on swear words and one brief sex scene. No one really objects to Orr's novel, partly because it's not as well known in the U.S. (though it has been published in many languages and with different covers), and partly because it doesn't have the bad words or references to sex as do the other two. Online reviewers of *Peeling the Onion* seem to love it or hate it, depending to some extent on those reviewers' own apparent disability status. Some readers of *Onion* may want Hollywood endings or poignant "overcoming a disability" stories, which *Onion* is not.

True Diary and *Onion* sharply critique society and the harm its assumptions can cause, but people don't necessarily interpret those novels from that perspective. And while *Stoner and Spaz* does not challenge society's harmful assumptions quite the way the other two novels do, it is a well-written book that provides a likable and witty protagonist with a disability, still a relatively rare character.

The Three Novels

Seventeen-year-old Anna, the first person narrator in Wendy Orr's *Peeling the Onion*, is on the way home from winning a karate tournament when she's in a car accident that will leave her with a permanent brain injury. This sudden impairment changes her relationships with her boyfriend Hayden, her family, her close friends, and mostly with herself as she must come to terms not only with her body's physical changes but especially with society's expectations of people with severe injuries. She also comes to see an unconventional young man, Luke, in a new way. The narrator of *Stoner and Spaz*, Ben, is a self-deprecating but witty sixteen-year-old with cerebral palsy who tells us about his friendship with the smart and witty Colleen, who is addicted to drugs but is also the first girl to treat him as a "normal" friend. *True Diary* is narrated by Arnold (Junior) Spirit, a fourteen-year-old living on a Spokane Indian reservation who sees that his dreams will not materialize if he stays there amid the poverty and hopelessness in that community. Arnold has what he calls in the first line in the book, "water on the brain," a phrase he amends later to call "hydrocephalus." It is a disability that continues to affect him, though racial issues and poverty take center stage in the plot. He decides to attend the white, rich Reardon High School, where he faces racist classmates, culture clashes, and faces a split identity. One way to gauge what cultural work a text is doing is to juxtapose it to other texts. To various extents, all three novels question received notions of what is expected, what gets defined as "normal," and interrogate societal myths. By looking at these three texts together, we can better see, as if in relief, the different cultural work they do.

The questioning of disability myths is not a common theme in mainstream fiction or in young adult novels in general. Nor is this questioning a primary focus in reception documents: published discussion questions, study guides, or quizzes, which focus on more conventional topics such as reading comprehension, plot structure, "close reading," symbolism, or reader response questions designed to get students engaged in the text. In fact, some reviewers of *Peeling the Onion*, as we will see later in this chapter, expecting perhaps a different narrative arc, appear not to "get" what that text may be suggesting about disability and society's beliefs about disability. While conventional questions can all accomplish worthwhile tasks in examining a text, locating specific "textual evidence," or sparking a class discussion, it's also critical that teachers or discussion leaders pose questions about how characters with disabilities are represented in the text.

The consequences of *not* challenging negative representations can be sobering. For example, in a study they conducted with pre-service teachers, Bruce Menchetti, Gina Plattos, and Pamela Carroll found that some young people develop their negative view of people with intellectual disabilities from reading *Of Mice and Men*. One of their respondents wrote:

> In *Of Mice and Men*, Lennie... acts just like a child...who does not know his own strength, which ends up being very, very dangerous. This is one of the reasons why I was scared of these particular people. I feared that they would try to touch me or grab me in some way and not realize their own strength or what they were doing. (59).

It's frightening to think of how many students today are studying this often required novel, dutifully hunting down plot points, metaphors, and themes, but not once being asked to think critically about the way this character is being represented and the harm such representation can do in the world outside the novel. As Menchetti et al. point out, even novels like *Of Mice and Men* can be used to draw attention to and even question negative stereotypes about disability—but only if critical questions are posed. It's important that teachers pose questions that might help students become "resisting readers" (Judith Fetterley's phrase) of a text such as *Of Mice and Men* that seems to perpetuate—if not launch—discrimination against people with intellectual disabilities.

Because the critique of ableism in Orr's novel is more subtle and yet more withering than that of the other novels, this chapter will focus on *Peeling the Onion*, comparing and contrasting aspects of *Stoner and Spaz* and *True Diary* throughout. Some readers may need help seeing the novel's critique of the status quo. Narrator Anna first passively accepts, and then begins to question, society's views of severely injured people. Over the course of the novel, Anna questions the role "trying harder" plays—and does not play—in healing. She also comes to change her definitions of "success" and "normality."

Early on, when talking about Luke, Anna still buys into society's definition of "normal," which does not include her: "He [Luke] doesn't ignore all my bandages and braces, he just acts as if I'm normal anyway; I don't mind him seeing me" (48). Note that she does not put "normal" in quotation marks to call the word into question, at least not in her narrative. Her narrative, although it's partially omniscient, is in regular print. This is in contrast to her inner monologue, which is indicated by italics. This inner monologue—dreamlike, fragmented, in thoughts she cannot reveal to her family or to readers—is juxtaposed to the more conventional narrative. Readers have to put the pieces together and see that she is fighting with herself about society's definitions and assumptions.

It is the rare novel that puts disability prejudices on the table for examination. Unlike *Of Mice and Men*, *Peeling the Onion* does call for this examination, though not in a didactic, explicit way. Although this novel seems to invite readers toward a more informed and less mythologized view of disability, readers do play some part in reading these texts in a receptive way. Because readers may be steeped in the same negative views of disability that the novel seems to question, they may need to be nudged toward critical thinking by questions that help them recognize harmful attitudes.

Complicating further how these novels may be received, all three narrators are, to some extent, unreliable: Anna because she is young, heavily influenced by her peers and her society, and also, early in the novel, heavily sedated by pain medication due to the severity of her many injuries. She also is not chin-up cheery after the accident, an attitude some readers may have been conditioned to expect from the severely injured: the idea that positive thinking will cure everything. Ben (age 16) and Arnold are also unreliable to some extent—Ben because he is self-deprecating and lacking in confidence, Arnold because he is even younger (14) and subjected to more traumatic family events than the others. Some readers may see the two male protagonists as more "likable" than Anna. They have a more straight-forward and accessible narrative style than does Anna, whose story of what is happening is interspersed with her deeply inner thoughts, indicated with italics, which often contradict—by design—the straight narrative. These juxtapositions do much to heighten our awareness of Anna's frustration and eventual rejection of many of society's dictates about disability, but some readers have found them difficult to follow, or misinterpret them as Anna's "whining."

All three narrators (Anna, Ben, and Arnold) find their new identities only after they question or reject societal myths about groups unlike themselves. These myths include preconceived assumptions about older people (Anna), notions about "tough" classmates and students of color (Ben), and assumptions about rich white students, particularly male athletes (Arnold). Anna learns what real friendship is (Jenny) and is not (Caroline). She also learns what real love is (Luke) and is not (Hayden). Ben develops agency. Instead of just watching old movies, he makes new films. And Arnold learns that some of his rich white classmates can be kind human beings, even if they do retain some lingering prejudices. In some ways, these novels are not so different from other YA novels in which protagonists on their journey to maturity learn things about themselves and others. But because disability plays such a central role in these texts, especially *Peeling the Onion* and *Stoner and Spaz*, and commonplaces about disability are so rarely questioned in contemporary classrooms, these texts are worth discussing at length.

Authors' Disability Status

While all three narrators have identity issues, the factors that contribute to these conflicts and how these conflicts are eventually solved have important differences, which may be related to the respective authors' disability status. The significance of these differences may be evidenced in the way the novels seem to "blame" different things for their characters' problems, and also in what each character has to "overcome" in order to find his or her identity. Ben's harmful self-image, for example, is not due solely to society's treatment of him or its judgment of his C.P. We are clearly invited to hold Ben responsible for not "trying hard" enough to join society. His grandmother's babying of him is also an easy target of blame.

In *Peeling the Onion*, one of Anna's conflicts is with herself, too, but in her case it's because she must grapple with strong, but invisible, assumptions regarding the supposedly miraculous benefits of "trying harder." When she tries as hard as is physically possible, and she is not "cured," she must come to terms with, and ultimately reject, society's judgments that have been inscribed in her head. To put it more simply, in *Stoner and Spaz*, it is the individual who must change and adapt to society, and in *Peeling the Onion*, it is society that needs to alter its views—of disability, of the "trying harder" myth, and the cure-all properties of "having a positive attitude." In *True Diary*, the critique is multi-faceted. Although Arnold's hydrocephalus causes physical problems, society's reaction to his stuttering and lisping exacerbates those issues. As the plot develops, however, Arnold's problems have more to do with other social problems. Like Ben, Arnold also changes his views of people and of society, but like Anna, he clearly sees the problems caused by societal assumptions, though he comments directly on the ones dealing with race, class, and gender.

It's possible that these differences in conflict and how they are eventually resolved may be related to the disability status of their respective authors. Like Harriet McBryde Johnson, the author of the novel discussed in Chapter One, the authors of *Peeling the Onion* and *True Diary* have impairments similar to their narrators. Wendy Orr was severely injured in a car accident, as was Anna in *Peeling the Onion*. The descriptions of what Anna endures, especially in the days and weeks immediately following the accident, are vivid and realistic. Sherman Alexie was born with hydrocephalus, as was Arnold in *True Diary*. Alexie has also identified as a recovering alcoholic, a disability that clearly interferes with the daily function of many of the characters in *True Diary*, including Arnold, though he himself does not drink. Ron Koertge, the author of *Stoner and Spaz*, was apparently non-disabled when he wrote that novel. On the back inside cover of *Stoner and Spaz*, Koertge tells us how he came to write about disability: "My wife works with the learning disabled, and the physically disabled. One night she came home and told me about a young man with C.P. —and a terrific sense of humor." In contrast, *Peeling the Onion* and *Stoner and Spaz* focus on a narrator whose disability is almost identical to its respective author's disability. The significance of this difference may be evidenced in the way the novels seem to "blame" different things for their characters' problems, and also in what each character has to "overcome" in order to find his or her identity.

"Trying Harder": Cultural Myths in *Peeling the Onion* and *Stoner and Spaz*

These two novels present a very different view of society's role in exacerbating an impairment. As Ben in *Stoner and Spaz* develops his new identity, he accepts the view that all he needs to do is "try harder," and the world will be accepting of him. Anna, however, in *Peeling the Onion*, matures by first struggling with, and then ultimately rejecting, that myth.

In *Peeling the Onion*, seventeen-year-old Anna is severely injured in a car crash. Her neck is broken—in what is called "a hangman's fracture" (12)—though the doctors don't discover the break at first, thinking it's just whip lash. This misdiagnosis leads to some close calls regarding further injury, first in how Anna's rescuers try to pull her from the wreck (she stops them, luckily), and then later when she is almost administered a type of anesthesia that would have meant moving her head and neck in a way that would have been very dangerous. Although the doctors do eventually discover the break, and it does heal (though not in perfect alignment), and Anna does regain some of her balance and coordination, this brain injury will result in permanent physical limitations, tinnitus, pain, and some cognitive difficulties.

However, one of the biggest obstacles Anna faces is a parade of cultural myths and catch phrases regarding disability: "Try harder," "You can do it!" and "Beating an injury," etc. A good part of Anna's maturation and finding of her new identity involves her gradual questioning of these myths, and her ultimate rejection of them. Readers also steeped in these myths may have a hard time with this narrative. Anna's view of these myths changes gradually over time, and we watch this happen through her sarcastic thoughts and the snarky comments she thinks but does not say. The narrative does not spell out in an obvious way Anna's critique of society's disability myths. It accomplishes this critique through a series of juxtaposed scenes and narrative shifts, which readers must interpret in order to see the critique. As rhetoricians know, an argument or point of view is more powerful when the reader or listener participates in putting together the argument and is actively involved in making the connections the rhetor suggests.[1] However, it's possible that some readers may miss the significance of the juxtaposed scenes and narrative shifts. It's also possible that some readers will see, even before Anna does, the self-righteous, judgmental and wrong-headed foolishness of some of these beliefs. Other readers may come to rethink these myths as Anna does: gradually. Some readers, if not prodded through discussions or questions, may never see it.

In her online blog about *Peeling the Onion*, Wendy Orr has written about how some readers take what the main character says at face value:

> As I was going through some of the notes that teachers and student teachers have sent me for this book over the years, it struck me that many of them, and most students, believe everything that Anna says—about her emotions and actions, which is good, because the point of her internal dialogue was to report as truly as she (or the author behind her) possibly could—but also about the other characters. And that's a problem. I love my Anna. She's a teenage girl fighting for her life and independence; at different times she's depressed, determined, overwhelmed, angry, bitter, hopeful, and occasionally many of these at the same time, or at least on the same day. People who are angry, wounded, and bewildered do not always make reliable reporters. (Orr, "The Unreliable Narrator")

Because Orr was in a car accident and received injuries similar to Anna's, her character's perspective on disability and society is perhaps more realistic and critical than the perspective of many of the novel's young readers, who may be inexperienced readers as well. That is why teachers can play an important part not only in posing questions about representations of disability in this and other novels, but also more pointed questions about plot structures, internal monologues, sarcasm, juxtaposition of scenes, and unreliable narrators. These latter topics should be familiar to teachers of English.

By the end of the first page, Anna has gone from a triumphant karate athlete celebrating a successful meet with her new boyfriend Hayden, to a young woman who nearly dies in a car accident. She is in and out of consciousness as she is taken from the car to the ambulance, the hospital, and surgery. She wakes up in a world of pain and confusion. She finds out, but not until quite a bit later in the book because of a misdiagnosis, that she has broken her neck, an injury that will leave her with some permanent injuries. Although early on in the novel she believes that she will fully recover in a couple of weeks—perhaps according to happy ending narratives she has absorbed—she slowly realizes that her life has changed forever. The ending is neither triumphant nor tragic. Anna learns that she will never be able to do some of things she loved to do before the accident, and she's not thrilled about that. She also learns, however, that her changed situation has brought into her life a new relationship with her family, new possibilities for a career, and new insights on her love life.

In order to develop her new identity, Anna must first confront, question, and ultimately reject society's binarizing of "normal" and "disabled." This binary is also firmly cemented in Anna's mind: She wonders: "When do you stop being normal and turn into a handicapped person?" (114). For Anna to mature and find a new identity, she must dissolve this binary. Early in the novel, she is having a bad time with this self-imposed dichotomy. That is, she has internalized the societal myth that cheerful strength can conquer all: "There are two Annas," she tells us. One of them follows what she calls "the rule" and "knows that if you're strong and cheerful and fight fair you win the game and live happily ever after" (16). "The other Anna," she says "is an amorphous blog who just *is* (16). This Anna, who lives with much pain and fear, "floats above and around and behind the cheerful Anna…" She fears that the second Anna "is the real me, but that can't be true, I won't let her, I've been the first Anna for so long, it's the only way I know how to be" (16). The ringing in her ears from the tinnitus makes it very difficult for Anna to read what she must in order to get caught up on her work. She tells herself, "*Ignore it; concentrate; what's happened to your willpower?*" (60). The old Anna is still firmly locked into the "Just try harder" myth.

The three poems Anna writes, one at a different stage of her identity development, show how much Anna changes over the course of the novel, as does her view of reality. Anna's English teacher has asked her to write a poem about herself. In the first poem, she describes herself as "Peeling like an on-ion," or like opening up Russian wooden dolls. The last two lines subscribe to the "happily ever after" ending that she knows everyone expects: "under the crepe and ribbons/ there's a perfect gift inside." But Anna knows this happy ending isn't true: "Which is a lie from one end to the other but might keep Martin happy" (93).

The second poem she writes shows that she is close to the lowest point of her identity building. She knows the first Anna is gone, but the second one has not appeared yet. Instead of the "perfect gift" inside the dolls, "the gift's stolen from inside." She explains that the layers are gone, but that "The real Anna doesn't exist" (120). She writes this second poem about five and a half months after the accident, just after Anna has seen a letter from the insurance company that has her categorized as "permanently impaired" (114). She agonizes over both words, asking herself, "Am I disabled?" At this point in the novel, about two thirds of the way through, Anna even wonders if she and her loved ones would have been better off if she had simply died in the accident. The "deal" she had made with God, to "get over it" in six months, is the "bargaining" part of the five stages of grief. The arbitrary time of six months is almost over, and Anna still has a long way to go. The third version of her poem appears on the last page of the novel, the very last text in the novel. The last stanza describes not a storybook "happy ending," but it shows us a new Anna, one who has hope for the future: "But under all the layers/ —a tiny green shoot sprouting—/ I'm growing from inside" (166).

Anna finds that ideas about disability are nowhere more powerful than in her own head. Society's "Get over it!" view is more subtle in the beginning because readers see the world through Anna's perspective, and in her old iden-tity, the "old Anna" keeps juxtaposing "normal" and "handicapped" or "dis-abled." One powerful myth cemented in Anna's head early on in the novel is that "beating" an injury or impairment or disability is simply a matter of the individual making up his or her mind to do so. She says this to herself: *"Beat-ing an injury is just a question of how determined you are, and I'm determined"* (34). When she cannot "overcome" her injuries through sheer determination, when the pain and the dizziness continue in spite of her "trying harder," Anna feels at first confused, betrayed, and depressed. She will become cynical and angry before she reaches, almost a year after the accident, a coming to terms with both what she's lost and what she's gained.

Another binary Anna has adopted from society involves either fighting completely or "giving in." About halfway through the novel, when positive thinking and faith healing do not work for her, Anna scolds herself in the italics that we know are her very inner thoughts. She's still reciting a version of the "never give up" myth, but at least there is a question mark at the end of her inner thought. *"I'll* never *stop fighting my injuries; what am I supposed to do—give in?"* (77). In the same way some of the angry campers in *Accidents of Nature* criticize the "never-give-up" emphasis on walking, no matter how much time and agony is spent on it, and finally fight off society's assumptions and decide that wheelchairs are much more efficient ways of moving about, Anna, too, at first resists using a cane and then finds that using one helps her immensely.

In her 2009 book, *Bright-Sided: How Positive Thinking is Undermining America*, Barbara Ehrenreich talks about how society's promotion of positive thinking can be used to blame people for their own financial or professional troubles: "The flip side of positivity is thus a harsh insistence on personal responsibility: if your business fails or your job is eliminated, it must [be] because you didn't try hard enough, didn't believe firmly enough in the inevitability of your own success" (8). She continues: "the promoters of positive thinking have increasingly emphasized this negative judgment: to be disappointed, resentful, or downcast is to be a 'victim' and a 'whiner'" (9). Society's expectations for relentless "trying harder" extends to individuals with disabilities. In fact, we can see some of these judgments in some book reviewers' estimations of Anna in *Peeling the Onion*, with one reviewer concluding: "whining about everything isn't going to solve anything" (Arastu).

In contrast, *Stoner and Spaz* seems to reinforce this happy faith in "trying harder." In that novel, it is not society's views of disability that hold Ben back; it is his own self-imposed lack of agency. While others occasionally call him names, and some of his classmates ignore him, society's views and practices regarding disability are not the main conflict in this novel. It is Ben himself, the individual, whom the text seems to tell us needs to "try harder" to join mainstream society, and society will happily embrace him. Society need not change. Ben must.

For example, on the opening page of *Stoner and Spaz*, we see right away something Ben will be blamed for throughout the novel: his lack of agency. As he tells us that he "limps" toward the movie theater, even that building seems to have more agency than Ben does: "Since I've been pretty much treading water all day, the marquee of the Rialto Theatre looks like the prow of a ship coming to save me" (1). The building seems to move, while Ben has been merely "treading water." Ben is always making self-deprecating remarks about his C.P., and in this opening scene he attempts the following joke with the ticket seller: "Since it's Monster Week, do I get a discount?" But the seller, Mrs. Stenzgarden, doesn't get it: "I don't think I understand, dear." We see, therefore, that Mrs. Stenzgarden is not judging him. She is portrayed as if she would never think of a person with a disability as a "monster," nor would the society she represents. It is merely Ben's self concept. Although Ben may have internalized society's estimation of himself in making that remark, readers are led to believe this bad attitude comes from the individual. He is the one who will need to change, as various characters will tell him throughout the novel.

Other factors related to disability are represented differently in *Peeling the Onion* than they are in *Stoner and Spaz*. Unlike the physical environment in *Peeling the Onion*, where Anna must contend with uneven paths and sidewalks, wobbly bar stools, and nurses who can't be found when she needs help getting to the bathroom, the physical environment for Ben is not an issue. He does have some problems getting in and out of cars (15), and he has trouble dressing or undressing quickly (33), but even the old Rialto Theatre seems to be fully accessible. In fact, he praises it for its decor: "It rained this morning, so I'm extra careful, but looking down at the tiles that lead to the big double doors isn't exactly a hardship. They are a very cool turquoise and black" (2). The problem that Ben must overcome is not society's treatment of him, nor an inaccessible physical environment, but his treatment of himself. As Ben begins to find his identity, and what is depicted as his main problem (his view of himself) begins to change, so do the verbs he uses as the narrator to describe how he moves.

Early in the novel, the verbs Ben uses to indicate how he moves emphasize his impairment. He is "limp[ing] past the cleaners"(1) and "dragging my foot" [down the street] (3). He describes himself as "gimping down the aisle" (5) and "lurching" across the street" (34). He says, "I'm going to move….But I don't" (7). He tells us he experiences "Life as an eavesdropper" (8) who is "lying on my cowboy bedspread with the remote in my one good hand" (20). Soon after he meets Colleen, the verbs get slightly more active: "The next day I find myself prowling the halls…Well, I don't prowl the halls, but at least I'm in the halls. I don't just go sit in my homeroom like a fungus"(26). He "darts" (52) and "strolls" (59) and "looms" (118). He even "steadies" Colleen (133) and "pushes back" against Colleen's troublesome boyfriend, Ed (155). Notably, about three-quarters of the way through the book, he does something he specifically said earlier that he didn't do. He "prowls": "As I prowl the halls the next morning…" (112). This depiction comes as he is developing his identity and following people's advice to be more involved and active. In fact, in the next paragraph after the "prowling," he says, "I stalk right up to her, and I mean it this time. Bad leg or no bad leg, I stalk" (112).

Ben does find a new identity and develops agency through the course of the novel. Ironically, he develops this agency through the badgering of Colleen, Marcie, and even some minor characters, who are all essentially telling him to "try harder," a philosophy toward living that seems to be a given in our society, but also seems to be an annoying refrain given by non-disabled people to people with disabilities. The message seems to be that society is pretty welcoming, if only people with disabilities would reach out, try harder, and get over themselves—and, of course, listen to non-disabled people's advice about how to live their lives. Anna in *Peeling the Onion* has a very strong reaction against that cheery command, as do Jean and Sara, as we have seen, in *Accidents of Nature*. In *Onion*, Anna receives good advice from Luke; however, she mostly comes to her own conclusions about how she needs to live her life. One of those conclusions is to reject some of society's assumptions about trying harder and what is "normal." And although one of Anna's former friends, Caroline, makes cracks that seem to blame Anna for Anna's physical difficulties, the text invites us to see Caroline as a shallow, clueless mean girl.

In *Stoner and Spaz*, we're invited to like the characters who tell Ben to try harder. Sometimes those exact words, "try harder," are used; other times that advice is the implied lesson in what people say to Ben, as if most of his problems in society are his own fault. When Ben mentions to Colleen that he's never been to school detention, she says, "What? You're not crippled, my friend. You're dead" (27). When Ben tells Colleen about a science fiction film he saw on television, she asks him, "Is that all you do–squat in front of the TV?" (28). Ben criticizes Colleen for being a drug addict, to which she replies, "You should watch who you're calling names. You're a f—ing loser who limps" (71). In other words he's a loser who just happens to have C.P. Their confrontation continues about who is to blame for their respective current situations. Colleen scolds Ben for blaming everyone but himself: "Maybe I'm a stoner, but the devil doesn't make me do it and my mommy and daddy didn't make me do it" (72). When Colleen calls Ben a snob, Ben replies that no one talks to him. She snaps, "And that's somebody else's fault?" (73). He calls himself "a spaz," whereupon Colleen starts to tick off on her fingers all the people with disabilities she knows who are successful in high school, ending this list with, "Get over yourself, okay?" (73). A few pages later, Ben scolds himself: "I don't try hard enough. I should talk to people more" (76).

Another person who scolds Ben is Marcie, the neighbor and "good mother figure" Ben never had, who helps Ben make his first film. She criticizes his attitude in her first conversation with him. When, still on Marcie's front porch, Ben makes a crack that he could entitle his autobiography *Ben, the Lucky Spaz*, Marcie says, "Why don't you come inside and be hard on yourself?" (35). At this point in the narrative, Ben is furious at her for this retort. Much later, however, Marcie is talking about Buddhist monks, and she translates part of their philosophy of life as being "not too hard on themselves when they screw up" (87). There is talk about not "wasting this incarnation" (87). The conversation then turns to people who have received heart transplants and how some of them continued their bad eating habits. Marcie wonders why some of them "had a chance to change their lives and they didn't take it!" (89). This comment hits Ben hard: "The hair on my arms stands up. I wonder if Marcie is talking about me, too" (89). Ben is also chastised by a minor character, classmate Stephanie, when he's interviewing people for his movie. She tells him he thinks he's "better than everybody else," and he denies it. She says:

> "Two years ago I asked you to run for treasurer of the freshman class, and all you did was glare at me."

> "You just felt sorry for me."

> "I needed a treasurer, and you're good at math." (119)

Once again, we are invited to blame Ben for feeling sorry for himself and for apparently imagining that his C.P. was isolating him from the rest of society. Again, the individual with the impairment is blamed for the problems encountered, not society. Although Ben's classmates occasionally call him the same names he calls himself, we are made to understand that they're quite welcoming and open to Ben. It is he who merely needs to reach out.

Stoner and Spaz does include some critiques of society's views of disability. Ben's peers sometimes ignore him, or they think of him as "better" than everyone else: "Brave and strong. A plucky lad" (10). This is the "inspirational" angle that many disability activists reject. (See, for example, Harilyn Rousso's autobiography, *Don't Call Me Inspirational*.) Ben also makes fun of the "triumph over adversity" theme in the film *My Left Foot* (11). But throughout this novel, the person who seems to contribute the most to Ben's disability is Ben, the individual. In *Onion*, Anna needs to change, too. But her movement is mostly against society's smug advice to simply "try harder," while Ben's movement is to embrace that advice. Anna also faces very real obstacles to becoming "normal" again, one of which is a very limited definition of what it means to be a "normal" person. All Ben has to do is reach out, and by the end of the novel he seems to be embarking on a promising career with the possibility of a new girlfriend. (Ben's story continues in the sequel, *Now Playing,* which is not discussed here.) While Anna finds her identity by shedding society's unrealistic definitions of "normal" and "disabled," and by rejecting the "just try harder" myth, Ben finds his new self by stepping up and embracing the "try harder" advice given to him by Colleen, Marcie, and others. It's noteworthy that Ron Koertge's short story, "Good Hands," in Don Gallo's *Owning It* collection, has a similar message about a disabled protagonist who uses a wheelchair and simply needs to "try harder" to make friends. In that story, too, society is portrayed as just fine.

As Anna develops her new identity, however, she must shed her unquestioning acceptance of society's bromides about positive thinking. Three-quarters of the way through the novel, Anna now becomes angry at the same "overcoming" myth she herself subscribed to earlier. When she and Hayden are out getting pizza, the server asks Anna why she's using a cane. Anna says only that she has injured her foot. The waitress replies, "That's a shame! Never mind—it's just willpower, isn't it? Think positive and you'll get there!" (98). Anna mutters to Hayden that she'd like a cattle prod for people who tell her to get over it by thinking positive and using will power. Her anger goes on to include those who subscribe to the "supercrip" trope, that is, people who "overcome" their disabilities and do feats unexpected of them. This myth is harmful because it makes it seem like people with disabilities who do not do things like climb mountains or hang glide are somehow slackers. Further, people are always telling Anna about people worse off than she is. Although Hayden says people are "just trying to help," Anna wants to give "three zaps for stories about one-armed swimmers, and ten for the next person who tells me about someone dying of cancer right after they broke their ankle!" (99). As Anna is bombarded with these well-intentioned mini-philosophies, she finds herself having to resist deeply ingrained, but invisible assumptions about society, sometimes called commonplaces in rhetorical theory.

Rhetoricians Sharon Crowley and Debra Hawhee argue that it is important for us to understand what commonplaces are and how they work. A commonplace is an assumption widely held to be true, even if it is not. "Some commonplaces are so thoroughly embedded in a community's assumptions about how the world works that they are seldom examined rhetorically"

(21). One example they give is, "Anyone can become president of the United States" (21). Without thinking about it too deeply, many people believe that commonplace, even though it may not be actually true. What's more, Crowley and Hawhee point out that our belief in these commonplaces may be "only partially conscious" (21), making them harder to examine for their connection with reality. For example, "Trying harder can overcome anything" is a belief Anna must confront and ultimately reject. Whether her readers get to that point may depend on what questions were posed and what was discussed during class.

Commonplaces are powerful because they are taken as givens. They are often used as warrants in building arguments and drawing conclusions, which is why people's logic is often wrong: because the primary warrant or premise on which they are basing their argument is an unquestioned, unproven, often mistaken, commonplace. These powerful, hidden assumptions may be what makes it so hard for Anna to come to terms with what's happened to her and to find her new identity; they may also be what prevents some readers from having the same kind of insight Anna eventually does concerning the falseness of these commonplaces—whether they are about disability, "trying harder," or groups of people.

The commonplace that Anna has internalized goes like this: Willpower, the use of "every ounce" of it, can overcome anything, even devastating injuries. This is a convenient belief for society because it puts the onus on the injured person to just get better. Those who don't get better must just not be trying hard enough to do so. It's a simple and convenient belief—for society—because it requires nothing from that society. At this early point in the novel, Anna still believes this cultural myth about her impairment. When "trying harder" doesn't work, she is at a loss for what to do.

Anna's internal rehearsals about "beating" an injury are followed immediately with short but powerful scenes of what all this "trying harder" is doing to her. She keeps much of her pain and dizziness from her family, but because of the interior monologue we're privy to, we can see the falseness of the "try harder" command and what it is doing to her. For example, when Anna comes home from the hospital, she tries to read and get caught up with her studies. But her brain injury is interfering with her ability to focus, and the tinnitus and the dizziness makes her almost pass out. But the messages she gives herself—italics in this novel indicating Anna's thoughts—reveal to us the societal myths about "willpower" that she's fighting. *I'm not giving in!* she thinks. But she can endure the agony only so long, and, knowing she will soon blackout if she doesn't get off that chair, she calls her mother to help her go to bed. Her final thoughts in this scene: *"But I tried—I really tried. I used every ounce of willpower. What am I supposed to do now?"* (60). This "blaming" of the person with a disability for his or her impairment can also be seen in the "self-help" books Jenny's mother, with good intentions no doubt, has Jenny bring to Anna: "I flip through the first one: meditation; understanding your motives for not being well—*motives?* What kind of motive could you have for pain?" (117). One book proclaims that a person has a reason for "choosing the particular injuries or illnesses that resulted. Only when you find that reason will you be able to heal yourself" (118). It is refreshing to see Anna's rejection of this nonsense: "I feel like throwing up—preferably on the book. 'Crap! What complete and utter crap'" (118). Anna's reaction to these books' absurd claims shows that she rejects these notions that she might have internalized earlier in her life.

Much later in the novel, on the second-to-last page, when Anna sees some of the good things in her life "that have happened because of it [the accident]," we see that she outright rejects society's pop psychology about accidents happening for a reason, usually to allegedly build the character of the person injured. Anna, in her new identity, is thinking for herself: "I can learn and grow from the experience even if I don't believe it was part of some cosmic training scheme" (165). Anna's rejection of this particular societal commonplace—that having an injury is a kind of planned regimen for making one a better person—is similar to Arnold's rejection, in *True Diary*, of a similar societal myth. In the same way Anna talks a lot about being injured, Arnold talks a lot about being poor. He explicitly rejects the societal myth that poverty is some kind of noble teacher and character builder. Arnold says, "Poverty doesn't give you strength or teach you lessons about perseverance. No, poverty only teaches you how to be poor" (13). Both Anna and Arnold must also reject society's views of themselves in order to find their respective identities.

If *Onion* is not explicitly critical of cultural myths, it does strongly imply that society needs a more enlightened view of disability. By juxtaposing the different reactions of minor but strongly drawn characters in the book, these different views of disability come into sharp relief. First, there is the very strong contrast between Anna's two best friends, Jenny and Caroline. Jenny sticks with Anna throughout her long recovery, while Caroline exits the scene early on. After Anna is home, Jenny and Caroline come to visit, and at first Anna believes that "life is normal again, gossiping with my two best friends" (44). But later, when Anna's shaking hands spill apple juice all over herself, she tries not to notice the look on Caroline's face and her horrified reaction to this small accident:

> ...she [Caroline] sat, frozen and embarrassed, totally unable to handle it. Sick and shaky is okay for hospital, but now I'm home I'm supposed to be me—me with broken bones, but not spastic. Caroline likes rules, and I've broken this one." (45)

The spilled juice incident is the beginning of the end of Caroline's friendship with Anna, who tells us that Caroline has not called "since the day she came over with Jenny" (50). Three pages later, Caroline drops in for a visit, and Anna is thrilled but "flustered" (53). When Anna asks if Caroline wants coffee, Caroline delivers this reply, "I've given up caffeine—it's amazing how much better you feel when you get all those toxins out of your system" (53). What's going on here is that Caroline is deeply rattled by Anna's accident and by the ongoing effects of the injuries from it. The giving up of "toxins" may be Caroline's attempt to control fate, to somehow ward off the bodily harm Anna sustained in the car accident, as if somehow Anna wasn't being careful enough. In a way, Caroline's announcement of her giving up of caffeine is a subtle way of "blaming the victim," a back-handed slap, as if it's Anna's fault, if not for being in the accident, then for not recovering from it fast enough. Indeed, this scene ends with this recitation of a cultural myth, and Anna's unironic pledge to herself: "If you want something badly enough, you always get there in the end" (53).

After the apple-juice-spilling incident, it was harder and harder for Anna to get in touch with Caroline. Anna calls her, but Caroline is always busy (55). Finally, after another phone call from Anna, Caroline comes over. Caroline chatters on about regular school gossip and what's going on in her life. When she says she thinks she might get the part of Nancy in the school production of *Oliver*, she talks about how it will be a lot of work but that she'll be able to do it. What she says next is a cutting blow that reveals why she's been avoiding Anna. Caroline views the tutoring and help Anna's been getting after the accident as underserved special treatment. In speaking about how hard she'll have to work if she gets the part in the musical, Caroline says: "Though they don't slack off the work requirements or give you any special help if you've got in-school commitments, not like when you're having a sickie" (65). Anna tells us how devastating this comment is: "It slides in and out like a knife; slipped in so sweetly, in the same breath with the gossip, that it takes me a moment to feel the sting. The savagery" (65). The short scene ends with Caroline passively refusing to set another social date with Anna. This end to the friendship is one of the lowest points so far for Anna.

The "special help" trope that Caroline casually drops on Anna hurts her feelings deeply. Later in the book the hurt turns to anger, perhaps a first step in her questioning of societal assumptions that Anna needs to grow into her new identity. She has just come from the occupational therapist, and Anna's shattered thumb is healing, but she still needs a variety of assistive technologies to compensate for her "shaky writing" (115). In a brief italicized inner thought, we see Anna realize what Caroline meant with her cutting remark earlier. We also see Anna's anger now in her sarcasm: *That's what Caroline meant about special treatment! Poor Caroline, having hands that don't shake*" (115).

There is nothing in *Stoner and Spaz* that approaches the depth of cruelty we see in Anna's friend Caroline in *Onion*. Although Ben in *Stoner and Spaz* does have to endure some mild name calling—with "spaz" being almost a term of endearment from Colleen—most people are kind and accepting of Ben, at least once he develops agency and confidence. The message seems to be that an individual need only get over his or her insecurities about disability, simply reach out to join the "normal" world, and the isolating effects of the disability will disappear.

Unlike in *Onion*, Ben in *Stoner and Spaz* has no real problem with barriers in the physical environment, no parade of strangers who give bad advice, and no friends who turn on him because of his disability. Although there are some minor characters who refer to Ben as "crippled," there are no outright cruel people like there are in *Onion* (Caroline and Nurse "Busy Butt"). These cold or clueless characters are similar to the rough physical therapists or creepy camp counselors described in *Accidents of Nature*, part of the non-disabled society that is not at all welcoming to people with disabilities. These characters' presence in *Onion* and *Accidents*, novels written by people with the same impairments as their protagonists, may tell us much about the way real people with disabilities are treated in the real world.

In Orr's novel, society's role is much more complicated than it is in *Stoner and Spaz*. Some characters are accepting and some characters are not. By juxtaposing these radically different attitudes, the text relies on readers to see the contrast and to critique the bad behavior of Caroline, the friend who is really not one. Later, long after Caroline is out of the picture, Anna and Jenny are discussing the reasons Caroline ended the friendship. Anna, who has been making very slow progress and gaining control of her limbs and her balance, is beginning to analyze Caroline's reaction to disability. Anna is also beginning to see society's expectations with some critical perspective. Anna says, "I broke the rule about getting better when I left the hospital" (94). In society's happy-ending narratives, hospitals fix patients, who then go home better or "cured." Anna didn't follow this pattern. Jenny, the good friend who becomes even closer throughout the book, adds further insight to Caroline's behavior, which is ultimately linked with fear: "...maybe it was safer to blame you for not being well, because if it wasn't your fault, then it could happen to anyone—even perfectionists" (94). Disability scholars have theorized that this fear is behind much of the prejudice toward people with disabilities in our culture. Visible disabilities remind people of their own vulnerability and mortality. Caroline was "blaming" Anna for her injuries, in the same way the self-help book projected culpability onto people with disabilities. If disability is the "fault" of the disabled, then all non-disabled people need to do is keep up their guard, resist becoming disabled, and thereby ward off age and death. It's a complicated formula, one that largely operates subconsciously.

Unless a novel becomes a rant or a sermon, which few readers want, the counter-hegemonic cultural work it does must have a degree of subtlety. This subtlety can be lost on readers who have never had to think about disability. In his *ALAN Review* article on *True Diary* and disability, Bryan Ripley Crandall has a number of good questions about YA literature and how it handles disability. His questions would work with many novels, including "classic" texts:

> Do power dynamics exist between able bodies and disabled bodies?
>
> Are characters with handicaps pitied? Promoted? Abused? Scorned? Celebrated?
>
> How does the setting affect characters with disabilities?
>
> What does the author intend to get from their able/disabled characters?
>
> How does the text define normal? Is the book's idea of normal different from your own? (77)

Here are further questions that can help students locate and judge harmful assumptions the text relies on or critiques in a subtle manner that not all students see:

- What internalized judgments from society must the narrator confront and ultimately reject?

- What assumptions about limitations on people in your society have you discovered?
- How might this novel be analyzed from a perspective that considers the role society plays in putting limits on people with disabilities?
- How does this novel challenge or confirm stereotypes about people different from the narrator? (Older people? People of the opposite sex? People from a different background?)

Sometimes "essential questions" (sometimes called "central focus questions" or "big ideas") can help readers compare and contrast a group of texts. Such questions can also spark discussions of disability and society:

- What makes a good friend? Or good boyfriend or girlfriend?
- What makes a good parent?
- How should one deal with misogyny or racism or ableism?
- How should one live one's life?

Questions posed about a text can help reveal the cultural work it is doing behind the scenes. Students will see these discussions as more important and engaging than the low-level plot-based questions typical of many worksheets and quizzes.

Changing Assumptions about Others

In all three of these novels, characters must change their views of other groups of people, a change of heart related, perhaps, to their changing views of disability. In *Stoner and Spaz*, Ben learns much about his classmates when he interviews them the second time for his film, when he asks better questions and listens to them. Anna and Arnold experience the most significant insights. In *Peeling the Onion*, it takes Anna almost a year to reject her internalized view of herself as a disabled person. She must confront and question other societal commonplaces as well: that older people are boring, asexual, and never use irreverent language. Arnold, too, in *True Diary*, finds he must change his mind about groups of people about whom society has taught him to have fixed assumptions.

Shortly after the accident, while Anna is still in the hospital, we watch Anna's mistaken assumptions about older people play out when her hospital roommates Ruby and Mrs. Hogan, both in their 80s, watch a pot boiler soap opera called "Sun and Surf" and proceed to discuss their desires and missed chances in life. Anna is surprised and shocked at their conversation. "Ruby is old enough to be the oldest hunk's grandmother—but she's obviously not thinking about knitting booties now" (19). Anna thinks of all-night discussions of sex she's had with her girlfriends, but, she says, "I never thought I'd be having a slumber party with eighty-year-olds and talking about the same thing" (20).

Another prejudice Anna must eventually toss out is her notion of a successful young man: that the successful young man does not wear his hair in a long ponytail, finishes college, and gets a job that pays well, regardless of whether or not it makes him happy. Luke helps her challenge that assumption. In order for Anna's mother to go back to work after Anna comes home, the family needs to hire a "reliever" (36), someone to help Anna when she goes out. That person is Luke, a young man and son of a friend of Anna's mother, whom she has already hired to help out in her mother's plant nursery. Luke wears his long hair in a ponytail, and he has left his program at college, where he had been studying business. Making assumptions about long-haired young men who drop out of college, Anna's father makes a crack about what kind of "plants" Luke might be interested in. Luke, too, recounts how someone at the nursery "jumped to conclusions at the sight of Luke's long hair and wanted to know when to transplant marijuana seedlings" (59).

Although she likes Luke, Anna, too, struggles to accept his view of life. In her mind, she questions his decision to quit school and take a low-paying job at her mother's plant nursery, plus this job helping her. She thinks of him as "just drifting" and judges his decision: "working in Mum's nursery could hardly be a long-term ambition" (56). But Luke says that "seeing where life takes you" is not necessarily a bad plan (56). Luke is not afraid to buck society's assumptions that every young man should have short hair, a college degree, and a plan. Anna has internalized this judgment, and she has not matured enough to resist it, as Luke has.

She wants none of that unplanned aspect of life, and she asks Luke how anybody can plan anything under those circumstances. We then get her internal monologue, in italics, with Anna's binary view of "normal." She can't stand "not knowing for sure exactly how soon I'll be back to normal and able to organise my life again" (56). Her assumption is that only "normal" people, people with no permanent injuries, can organize their lives. Anna has used this notion—that determination is all—to beat herself up before. It may be part of the self-loathing she's feeling because this widely believed myth has stopped working for her.

These clichés of "mind over matter" and "trying harder" may have come from, among other places, an attitude nurtured in Anna's beloved karate sessions. As Luke and Anna discuss the pros and cons of having an organized plan, Luke likens it to the "the difference in philosophy behind karate and Tai Chi" (56). Early in the novel, as Luke explains how the more "inner-directed" Tai Chi approach would see a rock in a river as something to simply go around, not break up. Anna's interior monologue shows us that she's still solidly locked into the societal commonplace that if people try hard enough, they can do anything. In one of the italicized sections, brief interludes that tell us what she's thinking, Anna rehearses this belief and how it applies to breaking bricks. She remembers how even though logic tells us that breaking a brick with a hand is not possible, that *you concentrate, visualize—and let loose and do it, do the impossible…*" (56). Whether we as readers are skeptical of this widely accepted saying depends on the extent to which we see Anna as a reliable narrator. As mentioned earlier, sophisticated readers are more likely to question that reliability than are developing readers, especially if they are steeped in similar sayings. If we rely totally on Anna for our view of this myth, it won't be overturned until much later in the book when Anna questions this and other commonplaces. Readers following the skillful juxta-positions of scenes, however, may reach that conclusion much earlier. Anna's rejection of societal myths parallels her change of heart about Luke and his philosophy of life.

Just as Anna comes to see Luke as well as her elderly hospital roommates in a new light, Arnold also finds that some people are more complex than he thought. Although football player Roger is the one who delivers the horribly racist joke on page 64, Roger is also someone who shows kindness toward Arnold later in the novel. Roger loans him forty dollars, doesn't tell the world that Arnold is poor, and generously drives him home. Arnold admits to him-self that people can be nice, if complicated:

And Roger, being of kind heart and generous pocket, and a little bit racist, drove me home that night.

And he drove me home plenty of other nights, too.

If you let people into your life a little bit, they can be pretty damn amazing. (129)

Arnold has other insights. Like Anna, he is always repeating unspoken "rules" or assumptions society has. The "rules" Anna grapples with mostly have to do with assumptions about disability, but as we have seen, she also comes to change her assumptions about older women, and men with long hair who drop out of college. Arnold knows only too well, for example, society's "rules" governing children who lisp. He also knows unwritten assumptions about gender: at what age boys must stop holding hands (age nine, see sketch on page 218) and when boys and men are allowed to cry "and not get punched in the face" (after having lost a big game in sports, see page 196). He learns something about society's limitations on girls, too, when Penelope tells him about her dream to travel the world and "to be remembered" (112). At first he makes fun of her, but then he comes around:

> And I couldn't make fun of her for that dream. It was my dream, too. And Indian boys weren't supposed to dream like that. And white girls from small towns weren't supposed to dream big, either.
>
> We were supposed to be happy with our limitations. But there was no way Penelope and I were going to sit still. (112)

As Arnold, Anna, and, to some extent, Ben learn to see in a new perspective the people they had previously stereotyped, readers, too, may be invited to think about the unfounded prejudices they themselves hold, including assumptions about disability.

Reception Documents on *Peeling the Onion*

To varying degrees, then, all three novels question conventional societal assumptions about disability and other issues. However, these seeds of critique need to fall on fertile soil. Readers encountering these challenges for the first time may need to be prodded to absorb the inferences. Sometimes novels need to be read twice. Sometimes readers need to be asked to think about their reactions. Some books may need the soil cultivated a bit by questions that get readers thinking. Otherwise, readers may come away from a book either not understanding it or having their prejudices confirmed.

A brief overview of some *Peeling the Onion* reviews on the web illustrates some of this "infertile soil" thinking. For example, one student review on the website BookRags.com seems to hold the very same societal view of simply "trying harder" that Anna must reject in order to find her new identity. This student writer complains that Anna "just gives up" and criticizes her for not having the "willpower" to continue reading or to "get better" (BookRags).

She discusses Anna's loss of Caroline as a friend, with no critique of Caroline's vicious remarks about the special treatment Caroline seems jealous of, or her snarky comment about Anna "having a sickie." At least on Wendy Orr's website, one question asks, "Why do you think Caroline acts as she does?"—which could open the possibility of a discussion of society's pressures regarding a "normal"/"disabled" binary.

Another student writes in her one-star (out of five) Goodreads review that Anna "just complained" throughout the story. This writer saw no growth in Anna and found the writing "confusing" (Arastu). From what she says early in the review, this student read the book on her own as part of a "disability unit" in an English class. It's likely, therefore, that she was reading it without discussing it in class and without any questions to help her navigate the book's unusual narrative structure, which she had trouble understanding. Significantly, she clearly had no guiding questions from her teacher to help her pick up on Anna's gradual questioning of some of the same assumptions this reviewer seems to hold. Another reviewer, also on the Goodreads website, just wants Anna to stop whining and get over her injury (though she says this in a more colorful way): "This book was horrible. SHE BROKE HER LEG GTFOVER IT AND MOVE ON. Goddamn this bitch was whiny" (Jenafer). This writer also seems to be a student.

These student readers are apparently coming away from this text with society's sometimes prejudicial views of severely injured people either further reinscribed or even more negative than they may have been before they read the book. Like the pre-service teacher quoted earlier who learned from *Of Mice and Men* to fear intellectually disabled people, these young readers need more preparation and/or more challenging questions to help them navigate this unusual novel. Where are the teachers' questions that might help these student readers see the critique of society that is at the heart of *Peeling the Onion*, even if the narrative doesn't hit us over the head with it?

Student readers are not the only ones who seem to be obliviously swayed by invisible societal assumptions. The writer of a *Kirkus* review, who at least put questioning quotation marks around a reference to a "normal" life, had trouble understanding the book, seeing the structure as "unconnected episodes" (Kirkus). While it might be argued that the short scenes are not connected with on-the-nose transitional sentences, the juxtaposition and contrast of the episodes is part of the point: Anna's developing critique of society's small attitudes. Readers seeing only this review, which completely leaves out the novel's subtle but activist view of disability prejudices, might see it as just another romance and bildungsroman.

Additionally, an online *Publishers Weekly* review appearing about two months after the *Kirkus* review begins with the same phrase, calling the novel "This Australian import." This reviewer refers to the loss of Anna's "normal appearance," with no quotations around the word *normal* to call its use into question, and seems to have the same view of Luke—calling him "a college dropout" —that was initially held by Anna's father before he got to know Luke. The reviewer inexplicably calls the writing "spare" and "flat," with no evidence to support that claim. The same reviewer accuses Orr of "careless mining of psychological platitudes," apparently missing even Anna's eventual bitter rejection of those platitudes ("Peeling the Onion"). This novel is not "mining" those sayings. It's skewering them.

Of the three YA novels discussed in this chapter, *Peeling the Onion* is the most critical of society and its notions about disability. However, although the book has received numerous awards, and has been out for a long time and published in a number of different languages, there are few discussion questions that invite readers to probe society's role in disabling people with severe injuries. Even Wendy Orr's excellent website, which provides questions and activities sent from teachers all over the world, does not emphasize this aspect of the book. There is a heavy emphasis on symbol, metaphors, and having students look more closely at word use. One activity asks students to "Look at the descriptions of pain on pp. 1, 2, 9, 18 and 52. Which one worked best for you? What key words are used which bring pain alive for you? What words do we associate with pain?" (Orr, "Teachers' Resources").

One question, however, does invite readers to consider larger issues. It asks readers to think about the reliability of the narrator, though it doesn't use that phrase:

> Writing in the first person gives only one person's point of view. Discuss whether the other characters are exactly as Anna sees or portrays them. Could there even be a difference between how she truly sees them and how she portrays them in the privacy of her own mind, i.e., the internal dialogues (Orr, "Teachers' Resources").

Asking readers to think about how the narrator portrays characters reminds readers that the narrator is a character, too. Although Anna at first accepts many of society's myths about normality and trying harder, it doesn't necessarily mean that we the readers are supposed to accept them. In fact, as we see the agony Anna is going through in trying to live up to these platitudes, we may begin to question them before this character does, but only if we don't see her narrative as 100% reliable. This nuanced critique of society, which comes partly through Anna as she develops over the course of the novel and partly through readers' observations of events, might be something the glib writer missed in the *Publishers Weekly* online review.

All reviewers, of course, are entitled to their estimations of a novel. And I realize I tred on the quicksand of older New Criticism to claim that I have the enlightened interpretation dictated by what's "in the text." It is a tenet of post structuralism that people "see" different things "on the page" or "in the text." But the plain speaker in me tells me that these reviewers just didn't get it.

Other reviewers, perhaps with more background in cultural criticism, or with more experience on the receiving end of thoughtless advice to people in pain, are quicker to pick up on Anna's ultimate rejection of society's benighted judgments. Another reviewer on *Goodreads*, Tawny, tells a story similar to Anna's regarding advice she received from friends to read when she had painful episodes of arthritis when she was in high school. Tawny, like Anna, was angered by some of the advice she read in self-help books recommended to her by friends. This reviewer says, "I'm so glad I was able to read this novel" (Tawny).

Another reviewer readily sees the assumption-busting work done by *Peeling the Onion*. Deanne Newton, writing on the website *Divine: A Community for and by people with a disability*, calls the book "relatable" and calls Luke a "life-affirming element"—unlike the *Publishers Weekly* reviewer, above, to whom Luke is simply a "college dropout." This writer sees the book showing how people with permanent injuries can still have "a new and positive future" that, she says, they can build "for ourselves" (Newton).

The last two reviewers mentioned have some physical similarities to Anna in that they have experienced severe pain or a long-term impairment. The student reviewers do not mention any such similarities, which is perhaps why those readers were not able to see the book's critique of conventional views of disability. I would argue, though, that all readers, like or unlike Anna, can be invited to understand the book's pushback against harmful stereotypes. Understanding that pushback can not only help students become better "close readers," though such close reading goes way beyond the conventional point-to-a-sentence-as-evidence drills practiced in much Common Core test preparation. Teachers or group discussion leaders might encourage more sophisticated understanding of inference by posing questions like the following ahead of time or along the way:

- What seems to be Anna's view of "normal"? As readers, to what extent do we accept this narrator's view of "normal"? What passages in the text indicate that Anna is expanding her definition of "normal"?
- What views of disability does Anna seem to hold? What are some of her notions about "being crippled" and what is "normal"? Where might those views have come from?
- To what extent is Anna a reliable narrator?
- In the beginning of her stay in the hospital, what assumptions does Anna seem to hold about older women? Why is Anna surprised at the discussion going on between her elderly hospital roommates, Ruby and Mrs. Hogan (pages 19–20)? What other examples force Anna to change her views of older people?
- What does Anna's father—and Anna, for that matter—first assume about Luke, based on the way he wears his hair, his clothes, and the fact that he has left the university?
- Karate teachers ask Anna to "do the impossible," (p. 56), mostly through "mind over matter." What message does this common phrase give to people? In what circumstances might that positive message have negative consequences?

These and other questions might help further the potential contribution Orr's book could have in making us all a little less oblivious to the powerful cultural assumptions that shape our views of ourselves and others.

Adding *True Diary* to the Mix

It is perhaps with the depiction of the protagonists' respective grandmothers that we see the starkest contrast between the cultural work done by *Stoner and Spaz* and *True Diary*. While *Stoner and Spaz* provides a likeable, humorous character in Ben, which shows readers that "People with disabilities are people, too!", it mostly lets society off the hook for needing to change its treatment of people with disabilities. The message seems to be that Ben can be as "normal" as he lets himself be and as his grandmother lets him be. In Koertge's novel, Ben's grandmother is described in masterful strokes, yet her depiction relies on stereotypes of older women. She "pretty much looks at everything like she has glasses-on-a-stick" (33). She makes him go to highbrow cultural events (36–37) and clearly disapproves of Ben's friend Colleen (16). Even when Ben's grandmother sits, "her spine [is] absolutely straight, the crease in her gray slacks sharp enough to cut your hand on" (36). Ben also says she looks "like an icicle in white linen slacks and a white blouse" (125). Although she does take good care of Ben when both his parents disappear, and she does invite him to talk to her about his problems (126), her overall attitude and her instant and continuing dislike of Colleen keep Ben from confiding in her. She wants what she wants for him, not what he wants.

Most of the descriptions about Ben's grandmother early in the book show her as annoying but harmless. However, we discover her most damning trait from Chana, a classmate Ben interviews for his film. She has seen Ben's grandmother distributing food at Thanksgiving, her hands covered by "little plastic gloves" (122). Chana does not think much of her, saying she has "One eye on that big-assed Cadillac of hers, the other up to Heaven where God's got nothin' else to do but put gold stars right next to her name" (122). In spite of the rich descriptions, the character of Ben's grandmother is nothing more than the cliché of the rich, white, older woman who is a racist. She is an easy target, her characterization a simple matter of playing to widespread cultural commonplaces about rich white women over fifty.

While *Stoner and Spaz* plays to stereotypes about grandmothers, *True Diary* disrupts those stereotypes. There is a whole chapter early in the novel devoted to Arnold's grandmother, as well as a loving and detailed sketch of her (68). Arnold loves her, she's funny and warm, and she gives him great insight on why Roger doesn't hit Arnold (because he respects him for standing up for himself) (68). Arnold tells us, "I love my grandmother. She's the smartest person on the planet" (72). Later, Arnold spends three pages telling us how wonderful his grandmother is, calling her "the most amazing person in the world" (154). In stark contrast to Ben's closed-minded and racist grandmother, Arnold's is the most open-minded person he knows. He tells us "the very best thing" about her, which he knows goes against prevailing assumptions about grandmothers: "She was tolerant. And I know that's a hilarious thing to say about your grandmother" (154). He continues:

> My grandmother had no use for all the gay bashing and homophobia in the world, especially among other Indians.
>
> "Jeez," she said. "Who cares if a man wants to marry another man? All I want to know is who's going to pick up all the dirty socks?" (155)

Alexie also reverses another tradition common in many YA novels, where parents are often depicted as abusive, clueless, or absent. (In *Onion* they are well-meaning but a bit clueless. In *Stoner and Spaz* they are absent.) Arnold tells us that his "mother and father are the twin suns around which I orbit and my world would EXPLODE without them" (11). They, too, have a touching sketch (12) that shows what they might have been had they had a bit more money and education. It's not that Arnolds' parents are perfect. They are both alcoholics. However, Arnold says his parents are "pretty good." They support his decision to go to Reardon High School. They go to his basketball games (143). They work hard to make sure he has money for lunch and new clothes occasionally (119). They talk to him. "And best of all, they listen to me" (153) —listening to their teenagers being an extremely rare quality in YA novel parents (See *Speak*). Although Arnold's father gets drunk every Christmas and disappears for a week, he goes to great lengths to save (in his boot) his last five dollars to give to his son (151).

This unusually positive characterization of a teenager's parents and grandparents complicates widespread assumptions both in the YA novel tradition and in American culture in general that older people are useless, old fashioned, overly cautious, homophobic, or racist. Alexie has been criticized for his depictions of fellow residents on the reservation as often being intoxicated. However, in this novel, there are many different "drunks," including his father's best friend Eugene, who was "funny and kind" (70) and beloved by his community. Alexie's YA novel challenges many prejudices in that it names and questions the written or unwritten "rules people live by" (Bruce, Baldwin, and Umphrey 123). Although *True Diary* does not focus on the narrator's disability to the extent the other two novels in this chapter do, its questioning of many community "rules" can, by extension, help readers rethink representations of disability. It fits with Alexie's view, quoted above, that books should "challenge, anger, and possibly offend" (Cline 197).

True Diary and *Onion* both work against harmful societal assumptions about particular groups, whether those groups are people with disabilities, boys who aren't allowed to cry, or white girls from a small town who have dreams of traveling the world. *Stoner and Spaz*, too, accomplishes some positive cultural work regarding disability. A character with cerebral palsy narrates the novel, and that character is funny, relatable, and develops agency as the story progresses, though as we have seen, he develops this agency because other characters tell him to. This book also reinforces some stereotypes, especially about rich, racist grandmothers and people with disabilities who don't "try hard enough." Ben's problems arise not because of the way society treats people with disability. If we blame anyone, we blame his mother for leaving him or his grandmother for over-protecting him. Sure, people don't talk to him or notice him, but Colleen and Marcie won't let him blame society for that. We're to understand that it's his fault; society need not change to make his life better.

Discussion questions found on the web do not ask students to challenge the novel's apparent message about Ben. The following questions are from a blog by Sara Lazarescu called "Sara Can Read," posted on June 6, 2013: The blogger writes that Ben "may be swimming in a small sea of self-pity" and that it "takes Colleen's brashness to force Ben out of his comfort zone...." The discussion questions seem to lead readers toward this idea that Colleen is the real agent of change:

1) Has he changed for the better? Has Colleen been a good/bad influence on him?
2) Do you think Ben would have found his passion for movie making without Colleen's support and why or why not?
3) Does Ben let his disability define him? How does or doesn't he?
4) What would you have done if you were Ben and met Colleen in the movie theater? (Lazarescu)

Other than the last question, which is a reader-response question designed to get students talking about their own lives as a way into the text, the other questions focus on Ben the individual, as if his problems are caused by his own attitude, which it takes an outside force, Colleen, to help him change. To be fair to this blogger, the text does seem to invite this view—that society is not at all culpable for the situation Ben finds himself in as a person with a disability.

Another online review, this one written by Matt Berman on the "Common Sense Media" website, summarizes the story as one in which "Ben...matures and is able to see himself in a new light." Again, it is only Ben's attitude that is the problem with his life. Society is innocent. The summary goes on to blame Ben further and to characterize Colleen as the agent of change: "...Colleen makes Ben begin to see how he's been wasting his life holding himself aloof from everyone out of self-pity" (Berman). The commentary goes on to say that Ben helps Colleen, too, but since Ben is the main character, it is significant that it is Colleen, and not Ben, who makes things happen in his life.

Stoner and Spaz remains one of my favorite YA novels. Well-written and fast-moving, with rich description and ironic humor, it has some of the best dialogue I've seen in this genre. I will continue to teach this novel because of its overall high quality and because it can start discussions about disability and society. When I teach it, however, I will now pair it with a companion piece, perhaps *Peeling the Onion* or *Accidents of Nature*, and I'll include some questions that complicate the "try harder" message it seems to deliver about disability, about the respective characters' conflicts, and where readers are invited to place responsibility for those conflicts. I'd also ask about what the implications might be for where that responsibility is placed, using questions like these:

- What do we know about Ben from the first page? How do we know this?
- Why does he make that comment connecting himself to a "monster"?
- What does that remark tell us about his view of himself?
- Where might Ben's view of himself as a monster come from?
- What kind of advice does Ben get from Colleen? From Marcie? From his classmates?
- To what extent are disabled people in real life included in social events with non-disabled people?
- What might be some real-world effects of a book like this that seems to imply that the world is a welcoming place for people with cerebral palsy, if only those people would "try harder"?

By contrast, in *Peeling the Onion* the society contributes much more to problems Anna is having. Some people are great to Anna. Although her family members develop various odd coping mechanisms for the changes they see in Anna, her relatives are warm and supportive. But some people are cruel: a few of the nurses, Anna's friend Caroline, and the authors of those ridiculous self-help books. Anna has real physical pain, extreme at times, but her psychic pain comes from how some people are treating her differently and how she sees herself as different. This difference between *Onion* and *Stoner and Spaz* may be partly due to the difference in disability status of the respective authors. Wendy Orr sustained injuries very similar to those of Anna, and she also had a long recovery time, as well as some permanent injuries. It is perhaps for this reason that *Peeling the Onion* seems to turn the critical spotlight back on society more so than does *Stoner and Spaz*, where Ben mostly just needs to become more himself in order to fit in. Anna, of course, must also change her view of herself, but in order to do that she needs to reject society's view of disability. She loses friends along the way, too, because of her disability—both

Hayden and Caroline. While Ben loses Colleen, it's because of her addiction, not his disability.

Talking about the cultural effects of a novel can help casual readers understand the power a text has to complicate or confirm stereotypes. Well-placed questions can help students not only resist harmful assumptions the text might be making about groups of people. Some traditionalists might argue that literature is to be appreciated and that to analyze its power over culture and policy in the real world is too "political." To that I would say that literature, like rhetoric, does its work whether analyzed or not. Texts that do not call into question society's view of disability (or other issues regarding how people are treated) simply reinforce the status quo. That reinforcement is also a political view, even if hidden in shared assumptions between writer and reader. Teachers can help open the curtain to reveal those assumptions. Students can decide for themselves if those assumptions are just.

Note

1. As Crowley and Hawhee point out in their book *Ancient Rhetorics for Contemporary Students*, this audience participation in making connections is what makes enthymemes so powerful.

· 5 ·

"NORMAL" TALENTS, RUDOLPH STORIES, AND "SUPERCRIPS"

In the tradition of the TV series "Monk," the bestseller *The Curious Incident of the Dog in the Nighttime*, by Mark Haddon, and, some would say, the Sherlock Holmes stories, several YA novels have a protagonist whose "disability" plays a part in solving a crime or unraveling a mystery. On the one hand, a sleuth with an impairment brings the disabled character out of the shadows and shows him or her in a positive light, foregrounding unusual talents or personality quirks that are valued in society, at least in this case. The qualities that might have once been seen as negative (obsession for detail, extreme logic, or intense focus) are in this situation seen as positive. These protagonists can show a world view, rarely seen in fiction, from these characters' perspectives. Typically, these detectives interact with non-disabled characters, and they all work as a productive team in unraveling the mystery.

On the other hand, this plot line runs the risk of suggesting that the character's impairment, quality, or talent is somehow superhuman. The stories can become tales of "supercrips." In his book *Disability Rhetoric* Jay Dolmage refers to Joseph Shapiro's concept of the "supercrip." As Dolmage explains, this character is part of an "overcoming or compensation" disability myth:

> In this myth, the connection between disability and compensatory ability is intentional and required. The audience does not have to focus on the disability, or

challenge the stigma that this disability entails, but instead refocuses attention toward the "gift." This works as a management of the fears of the temporarily able-bodied (if and when I become disabled, I will compensate or overcome), and it acts as a demand placed upon disabled bodies (you had better be very good at something). (39–40)

Beth Haller also points out how what she calls a "Supercrip Model" is harmful: "This representation reinforces the idea that people with disabilities are 'deviant'—that the person's accomplishments are amazing for someone who is 'less than complete'" (Haller). The result is that people with disabilities, including "supercrips" and those who have not "overcome" their impairment, are all seen as "other."

The characters in this chapter are not superhuman heroes, but they have developed skills, perhaps because of their life experience, that can contribute to society. In their review of Paul Longmore's book, Smith and Erevelles write:

One means of countering the dehumanization of disabled people is to encourage non-disabled society to recognize that disabled people have both a history and a culture that contribute in transformative ways to both disabled and non-disabled society. (35)

While the novels discussed in this chapter do not explore disability histories, as Longmore calls for, they do, however, emphasize the contributions these characters make to society. Although it can be a fine line sometimes between harmful "supercrip" stereotypes and more modest talents or intellectual habits developed by the disabled characters in these novels, teachers or discussion leaders can pose questions that will help readers explore the more sophisticated yet overlooked ways in which people with disabilities contribute to society.

I examine four mystery novels in this chapter, all of which have a detective with a disability. The first two, *The London Eye Mystery* by Siobhan Dowd, and *Marcelo in the Real World* by Francisco X. Stork, both have a narrator on the autism spectrum. In the third one, *From Charlie's Point of View* by Richard Scrimger, the detective is blind. In the fourth, *The Dark Days of Hamburger Halpin* by Josh Berk, the person who solves the mystery is deaf. Because they employ what might be seen as an almost super-human ability as they solve their respective mysteries, these characters raise the specter of the "supercrip."

I also explore these novels through what I call a "Rudolph the Red-Nosed Reindeer" concept (of children's Christmas song fame) because, in the end, the individual who was formally mocked, bullied, or ignored becomes a hero who saves the day. Like Rudolph's bright nose, which lit the way on that stormy night when the others could not see, the protagonist's difference plays a key role in solving the mystery. However, even though these protagonists may no longer be ostracized as burdens or objects of ridicule, they still may not be seen as fully human. Yes, their differences are now celebrated, but these differences still set them outside constructed notions of "normal" in a society that has not changed.

In addition, these stories can imply that it is always a desirable thing to be a part of "normal" society and that society is just fine the way it is. While other members of society, like the other reindeers who used to laugh and call Rudolph names, are now the ones who learn to see these protagonists in a new way, they do so because this character has done something amazing that helps them out, as Dolmage describes above. Definitions of "normal" may not ever be questioned or expansions of that term put forward. Society's assumptions may not ever be challenged. The original "Rudolph" song certainly doesn't suggest anything ought to change or that there's something wrong with that society. It never advises, for example, that the reindeers ought to stop their name calling or give Rudolph a turn in the reindeer games. It is the individual, Rudolph, who has to prove himself.

What's wrong with characters with impairments being heroes? One implication of this narrative, if not identified and challenged, is that a "successful" disabled person can't just simply be, can't just live a normal, satisfactory life without being expected to develop larger-than-life abilities which become a ticket to acceptance. Simi Linton has critiqued the "overcoming" language regarding disability: "An implication of these statements is that the other members of the group from which the individual has supposedly moved beyond are not as brave, strong, or extraordinary as the person who has *overcome* that designation" (18). Others have pointed out this and other dangers of stories in which a character with a disability "saves the day." Drawing on critiques by other disability scholars, Arndt, White, and Chervenak describe how similarly questionable messages appear in another medium—film. They warn that films about disability run the danger of "sending the message that inaccurate or exaggerated stereotypes about disability are accurate and acceptable" (Arndt, White, and Chervenak).

They specifically analyze two films, *The Mighty* and *Simon Birch*, which they say perpetuate stereotypes of people with disabilities as "both pitiable and heroic." They point out that it is harmful to watch such films without active critical analysis of the messages these films promote, which is that the characters with disabilities (in this case, Morquio syndrome) be seen "as both selfless heroes and pitiable individuals, whose heroism and sacrifice emanate directly from their 'afflictions.'" Arndt, White, and Chervanak also criticize these films for using "disability as a major—or even sole—facet of Simon and Kevin's characters; it is their disability that drives the plot and informs their roles as innocents and superstars, then, finally, tragic victims." Kevin, in *The Mighty*, saves the day by using his crutch to reach the gas pedal of a van, slides down a steep hill, becomes airborne, and manages to cross very steep terrain in his quest to save Max from his murderous father. However, his superhero actions take a toll on his body. He weakens and dies shortly after that stunt. These films can be especially dangerous, these authors point out, when they are viewed with no follow-up questions that ask students to examine critically the way disability is constructed. Therefore, teachers and students should discuss together the pros and cons of how the main characters are portrayed in such films and in novels with similar themes, and these discussions should be informed by the theories and voices of people with disabilities. Keeping in mind the "supercrip" or superhero danger raised by Dolmage, Haller, and others, as well as the "Rudolph" concept I've explained above, let's examine these four YA mysteries.

The London Eye Mystery

Siobhan Dowd's award-winning YA novel, *The London Eye Mystery*, was published in 2007, right before her death from breast cancer at age 47. According to her obituary in *The Guardian*, she began work on *London Eye* in 2003, the year before Mark Haddon's novel, *The Curious Incident of the Dog in the Night Time*, was published and became a bestseller. Because Dowd's book, too, was a mystery solved by a young man with Asperger-like characteristics, she worked for a while instead on another novel and finished *London Eye* later (Fryer).

   London Eye is narrated in the first person by 12-year-old Ted, who has a "syndrome" which is never named, though he describes his brain as running "on a different operating system." His hands "shake themselves out," he jumps on his bed "to clear his mind," he has trouble looking people in the eye, he has a hard time with small talk, and he does not like to be hugged. He is extremely interested in weather patterns and systems. Ted wants to have friends and wants people to listen to him. He's also extremely logical, focused, and in the habit of looking at things from a different perspective. His sister Kat tells him, "Nobody's better at thinking than you are" (74). His cousin Salim comes to visit the family with his mother, Ted's Aunt Gloria. One day Salim takes a ride by himself in the London Eye while Ted and his sister Kat wait for him on the ground, watching Salim's pod make the thirty-minute rotation high over London. When the children don't see Salim get off his pod when it gets back to the ground, they begin the long process of figuring out what happened to him.

Ted tells us that his "funny brain that runs on a different operating system from other people's helped me figure out what happened" (4). This "syndrome" gives Ted a different perspective on the world, much like riding the London Eye gives riders a different perspective on the city below. The "depending on how you look at it" refrain and the recurring references to what a different perspective can offer refer to many things: the view of London from the Eye, the clues surrounding Salim's disappearance, Ted's "syndrome," as well as the assumptions of the society in which Ted is considered not "normal."

Ted's "syndrome" is not the subject of the book. The mystery is. But it is Ted's unusual logic, attention to detail, and different perspective on the world that help him solve the mystery. His fascination with weather helps him with his analysis, as does an analogy he makes between Salim's case and the "Coriolis effect" in weather, "the difference between…two tangential velocities," the variable that results in the fact that "If you throw something from the equator toward the North Pole, it won't go straight, but crooked" (205–6). Ted figures out an analogous "deflection" that might have kept Salim from coming home (299). With this premise, the novel could have easily slipped into "superhero" mode, and it does have elements of a "Rudolph" story: the family that mocks Ted comes to respect him after he solves the mystery. However, the novel is not as simple as that. Ted's likable but imperfect sister Kat is highly active in solving the mystery as well, and Ted needs her bravery, her quick action, and her ability to read body language. She needs his analytical thinking. They work as a team.

More significantly, this novel also examines, in a positive, hopeful, but definitely critical way, the society in which Ted finds himself ridiculed, bullied, and excluded. Like others in its genre, the mystery has an unlikely plot, but this book is not naive. We learn that "the rough boys" routinely bully Ted on the playground (76), and Salim and his friend Markus are both bullied at school for being non-white (279–80). The book also repeatedly challenges judgments of what is "normal" and emphasizes the value of different perspectives. In spite of its warm humor and mostly likable characters, including parents and other adults, the novel also includes some serious critiques, not only of what is considered "normal," but of society in general.

For example, a tall building that will play a big part in the mystery, Barrington Heights, is called the "Barracks," a place where, as Ted explains, "socially excluded" people used to live. What follows is a long social critique, not of the people who lived there, but of the society that played an active part in creating the situation that put them there:

> Being socially excluded is a bit like being excluded from school. Instead of a head teacher telling you you have to leave, it's more that everybody in the rest of society acts like you don't exist. And you end up with all the other people who are being ignored. And you're so angry that society is treating you like this that you take drugs and shoplift and form gangs in revenge. And the people in Barrington Heights used to do all those things. Dad said it was not that the people were bad to begin with. He said the building was sick and made them sick too, a bit like a virus. (10)

This view of poverty and crime may be a reflection of Siobhan Dowd's many years working with underrepresented groups before she started her writing career. In the first paragraph of her obituary in *The Guardian* she is described as a "writer and human rights campaigner" who was "passionately committed to countering oppression and discrimination." One of her last acts before she died was to set up the Siobhan Dowd Trust, which provides books for "young people in areas of social deprivation," as the back inside book cover describes them. What is stated explicitly in the above passage about the role society plays in encouraging crime, is, by extension, what this novel seems to argue implicitly about the role society plays in disabling people, in contributing to whatever it is that Ted "has." In maintaining such restrictive definitions of "normal," society excludes a smart, logical boy like Ted, who is made to feel like he has something wrong with him. Ted has a difficult time fitting in, partly because he has trouble reading people's facial expressions and he has trouble understanding some idioms, but mostly because society is not open to his different way of being.

"Normal" society is problematized throughout the novel. Although the book is light-hearted and pleasant, there are some realistic scenes that depict the harsh realities of life in modern society. When Salim goes missing, Kat fears that someone may have kidnapped him for sexual reasons. A young Asian boy is found dead in the Thames, and for a few hours the family fears it might be Salim. It turns out not to be him, but the fact that one young man, homeless and alone in the world, has lost his life clearly haunts Ted and Ted's father, who had the task of going to the morgue to see if the boy was his nephew.

There are several fine lines books like this must negotiate if they are to challenge destructive assumptions about disability without turning characters into "supercrips" or Rudolph figures. I do believe this book, this author, was trying to challenge those destructive assumptions. The novel stays, for the most part, on the productive side of those lines. However, it's difficult to challenge assumptions without being didactic and without being able to predict what all readers will "get." The protagonist with the "syndrome" has to have characteristics that readers will recognize as being different, without crossing over into cliché or reinforcing stereotypes. Some of the person's features must be different enough so readers see why the character and his community have trouble adjusting to each other (the hand flapping, the inability to look people in the eye, the literal mindedness). Yet some of that character's qualities need to be described in a way to be seen as positive, as contributing to society in a way that other characters cannot—but in a way that does not make the person seem like a superhero, because superheroes are not full members of society, either. And turning a disabled person into a "supercrip" can give the impression that people with disabilities must demonstrate some unusual, world-saving feature in order to be valued by society.

Ted comes close at times to being such a character, with his particular talents solving the mystery and possibly saving the life of his cousin Salim. His sister Kat is the first person to see the benefits of his logic, focus, and "different operating system," and about halfway through the book she calls him a "genius" (171). But we as readers, who are now identifying with Ted as he narrates the story, see him as sensitive and smart—certainly within "our" definition of "normal," if not the definition of the characters in the book who are ignoring him—the same way the people in the Barracks are ignored.

Ted himself, the 12-year-old narrator, is already questioning society's apparent view of his "syndrome." When Ted's Aunt Gloria is talking about Andy Warhol, she blurts out that the artist may have had "what Ted's got" (30). This statement does not sit well with Ted's mother, but Ted comments to readers:

> Mum's lips pressed up tight...But I didn't care. I know I'm a weirdo. My brain runs on a different operating system from other people's. I see things they don't and sometimes they see things I don't. As far as I'm concerned, if Andy Warhol was like me,

then one day I'd be a cultural icon too. Instead of soup cans and movie stars, I'd be famous for my weather charts and formal suits and that would be good. (31)

In a conversation with Salim, who asks Ted about "this syndrome thing you've got" (36), Ted explains a bit about it, including that he used to jump on a trampoline to help him think. He continues: "My syndrome means I'm good at remembering big things, like important facts about the weather. But I'm always forgetting small things, like my school gym bag" (37–8). We get some insight into Ted's mixed feelings in this conversation with Salim, when Ted tells him something he's not told anyone else: "I don't like being different. I don't like being in my brain. Sometimes it's like a big empty space where I'm all on my own. And there's nothing else, just me" (38). Yet, Ted knows himself and is mostly happy with himself. He tells us, "I am good at counting things and timing things and remembering things (91), and "I am good at looking at things differently" (161). At one point before the novel opens, Ted was hoping for a "cure," for his "syndrome," which he had asked his mother about when he was younger (199). But it's clear that in the present time he is no longer hoping for a cure; nor does he want one.

The novel suggests that while Ted and his family do not consider him to be "normal," "normal" is also not seen as something that is completely desirable. "Normal" people lie, which Ted learns to do. When Kat learns that Ted has lied a second time, she says, in her own slam at society, "One of these days you'll be nearly normal" (220).[1] Ted lies three times during the course of the novel. This new experience of lying also helps him see that when Salim's friend Markus, who turns out to be in on Salim's disappearance, said that he was out with the scouts, that he could have been lying. This new insight plays a big part in helping to find Salim. Ted also gets better at reading body language, but he mostly relies on Kat to read body language and believes her readings. Meanwhile, she gains a new respect for his analytical skills. Although Ted gets most of the credit for "working it out," he publicly acknowledges Kat's help: "I'd never have worked it out without you, Kat" (278).

Just before the mystery is completely solved, Kat and Ted reach the same conclusion that a key player they've just spoken to is lying. Kat no doubt can read the man's body language, and she, like Ted, needs to isolate herself (by riding around and around on a scooter) and think. Ted's new ability to lie helps him a bit to see the man is lying, but he also uses a weather analogy. He sees the man as a "mini Coriolis force trying to deflect us" and he also uses his "deductive thought" to compare the two different stories the man told

(227–228). What's important about this scene is that Ted is not seen as a superhero or as particularly unusual. He and Kat are pooling their talents to run down this lead. Their "minds had met" (227), and they had each learned from one other. This scene suggests a broadening of the term "normal" to show how Ted's thinking patterns are not outside that realm. The scene suggests that it is society that makes Ted feel he is different, not his habits or his brain. By working together, the two children move further along in solving the mystery.

What overall impression, then, does *The London Eye Mystery* leave us with? How does it represent disability and society's role in disabling individuals? Society is criticized without the text relying on stereotypes about Ted's character or about other characters. (As we will see later in this chapter, some authors do seem to rely on stereotypical, even misogynist descriptions, especially for female characters.) Although Ted's Aunt Gloria is a bit hard to take at times, she is good hearted and she does change and become more open to her son Salim's wishes about moving. Although his family does not listen to Ted, even when he says he's figured out how Salim got out of the pod, the police inspector, a woman, does listen to him.

Society is strongly criticized in an explicit way for its treatment of poor people and in an implicit way for its treatment of young people like Ted. Clues are given throughout, so the plot has no *deus ex machina* moves, but it's not completely obvious what happened to Salim (at least, it wasn't obvious to me). The novel has a warm, humorous tone, though there are scary moments when characters are affected by real dangers and tragedies in the world.

We're clearly invited to see how wrong Ted's family is for not listening to him. But they love him and he's a full member of the family. His parents are flawed but also loving and witty. Ted's older sister, Kat, is a typical sibling in the sense that she can ignore him or not listen to him, but she also does take his theories somewhat seriously, at least some of the time, and she does respect him in the end. Although it is Ted's thinking and analysis that "works out" what happens to Salim, it is Kat who acts on things and runs off to hunt down the "strange man" who turns out to be Markus Flood's cousin, who helps Salim and Markus with the ruse. So Ted is not the lone "Rudolph" who solves things completely by himself, though clearly the characteristics of his "syndrome" have played a big part.

Why have students read a book like this, other than for its substantial entertainment and literary value? First, if a young reader has no background knowledge of "syndrome" like Ted's, and suddenly has a classmate with similar behaviors, this novel might make that young reader think twice before, say, bullying that person. Second, it might also help readers with some of Ted's qualities feel less alone. This novel does run some risk of drawing on stereotypes or giving the impression that all people with Ted's "syndrome" have his talents and characteristics. However—and this is the third reason—it's also a step in a more respectful direction for a general public that might have far more negative or "othering" assumptions. Ted is likable, smart, and very "normal" in many more ways than he is "other." The message this novel promotes is that people with this "syndrome" have much to contribute to society, *and* they are "normal."

Teachers using this book, however, should help students consider the tightrope authors must cross to write these books responsibly. Paul Heilker and Melanie Yergeau raise a question that might be relevant in such a discussion: "…how meaningful—and to whom—are the distinctions between people on the autism spectrum and those who are often presented as their polar (and more desirable) opposites, the neurologically typical?" (486). Who gains and who loses by categorizing a person like Ted and making him feel bad about himself? The drama of this novel comes close to posing that question implicitly, so these scholars' explicit phrasing of it would be a good question to use in group discussions of this text.

Another question might be, "What's the problem with having a person with a disability be the one who saves the day because of his or her special talent, which is the result of the disability?" A discussion of this question might reveal that such a representation can suggest that it's not enough that people just live their lives, which have value without a special talent or "gift" playing a part in solving a dramatic mystery. Such representations suggest that in order to be invited into "normal" society, they need to become heroes or super solvers of crimes. Handled poorly, these stories can leave readers with the message that individuals with Ted's characteristics had better find a way to use those odd talents in a way that helps "normal" society. On the other hand, some "Rudolph" stories, if they're not too unrealistic, can draw attention to the strengths and talents every individual has, instead of allowing people to focus only on the "impairment" or perceived lack of something that "normal" people have. Done carefully, these stories can expand definitions of "normal" and invite society to look at itself and how it might improve. I believe *London Eye* falls solidly into the latter category, providing some serious but not heavy handed critique of a number of problems in society. To safeguard against the "superhero" or "compensation" myth, however, teachers can pose questions and open discussions about stories that veer too close to the superhero line.

Marcelo in the Real World

Another YA novel in which a character solves a mystery is Francisco X. Stork's *Marcelo in the Real World*, which won the Schneider Family Book Award (teen category), an award which honors a book "that embodies an artistic expression of the disability experience for child and adolescent audiences" (from their website). The book opens with Marcelo, the first person narrator, undergoing a test that looks at his brain waves as he hears what he describes as "internal music." We infer from the doctor's comments and from the narrator referring to himself as "Marcelo" in his conversation with the doctor, as well as his comments on reading facial expressions, that Marcelo may be on the autism spectrum, though Marcelo's explanation of his characteristics does not come up until later. The first time Marcelo tells us about his tests, he questions his own need for them. He says that the doctor is gathering information for "other people who truly need help," implying that he does not.

Like Ted in *London Eye*, but older, Marcelo, who is 17, has qualities similar to Ted's, though autism-related categories are actively questioned throughout the novel, and the definitions of many terms like "normal," "disease," and "illness" are repeatedly challenged by Marcelo and others. And the "real world" in this novel, like the unequal society depicted in *London Eye*, is seen as corrupt and in need of reform. In the same way *London Eye* pointed out the damage done by society ignoring certain groups of people, *Marcelo in the Real World* exposes the difficulties "seven Mexican-Americans at Harvard Law School" faced when Marcelo's father Arturo went there (189).

Like Ted, Marcelo has trouble with "small talk" and learns to lie. Both have trouble with figures of speech, dislike being touched, and want to have friends. Both have supportive older sisters, though Yolanda, Marcelo's sister, is a minor character. While Ted's hand is always "shaking itself out," Marcelo can control his arm movements most of the time. Once, when he's having a difficult conversation, he tells us "my hand is opening and closing automatically. I stop it from doing that" (165). Both Ted and Marcelo notice details in documents or photographs, a talent which plays a small part in solving their respective cases. Also like Ted, Marcelo does not work alone, though in each case it is the narrator's "special interest" that plays a big role in unraveling the mystery. Marcelo's "special interest" is religion, which, like Ted's deep knowledge of weather patterns, helps in the resolution of the conflict.

Marcelo's father, Arturo, insists that his son work at his law firm over the summer, in order to learn better how to live in what he calls the "real world." He would like Marcelo to attend "a regular high school," but Marcelo desperately wants to stay at Paterson, a private school for students with disabilities. The deal is that if Marcelo succeeds at the law school job over the summer—though it is his father who will define "success"—Marcelo will be able to decide where to spend his senior year. While cleaning up an office at the law firm, Marcelo discovers a photograph of a young girl, Ixtel, whose face was maimed by a faulty windshield, produced by a company his father is defending in a lawsuit. Some key evidence in the case has been removed, and if Ixtel is going to be able to get the surgery she needs to reconstruct her face, her lawyer will need access to that evidence.

Marcelo's main conflict is not focused on his alleged disability. He has internal conflicts: he must decide whether to help the evil Wendell to "get" Jasmine, his young co-worker with whom he develops a friendship and a possible romantic interest. And then he must decide whether to help his father or Ixtel:

> I feel an obligation to right my father's wrong. But why? Shouldn't my father's welfare come first? His welfare is my welfare. How does one weigh love for a parent against the urge to help someone in need? (252–253)

It is Marcelo's keenly developed sense of morality and his philosophical musings that help him pursue the mystery and reach a decision about how to act. He does decide to turn over the evidence, which will help Ixtel but will greatly embarrass his father's law firm. At the end of the book, Marcelo knows he cannot return to Paterson because "he did not succeed in following the rules of the real world" (289). Readers will understand, however, that the rules of the real world are suspect, if not corrupt, and that Marcelo has succeeded in a way that his father's law firm will not define as success. He is operating under different, in this case more moral, rules.

Marcelo is not a superhero, but this novel has elements of the Rudolph story in that the character who was mocked or underestimated in the beginning is the one who comes through in the end. Marcelo discovers the corruption in his father's law firm and pursues evidence that will re-establish justice. He saves the day for Ixtel. But he does have help. Just as Ted has Kat, who is the active leader in the *London Eye* case, Marcelo has Jasmine, who actually locates the important file Ixtel's lawyer needs.

Also unlike simple Rudolph tales, this novel is highly critical of society. Definitions are challenged; terms are qualified. Early on in the book, when

Arturo is telling Marcelo that he hopes he will go to the "regular" high school in the fall, he implies that the life at Paterson is neither healthy nor normal, "There is life out there that is healthy and normal that you need to be a part of" (23). This statement becomes ironic fairly quickly as we learn about the questionable motives of Arturo's law partner, Stephen Holmes, his son Wendell, and even Arturo himself. Marcelo has always believed that his father "always does what is right" (166), but readers can see early on that that's not the case. Even before Marcelo learns about all the evil in the world, however, including what he will learn about his father in the novel, he questions his father's definition of "normal":

> Atruro is basically asking me to pretend that I am normal, according to his definition, for three months. This is an impossible task, as far as I can tell, especially since it is very difficult for me to feel that I am *not* normal. (23)

He also takes issue with his father's view of the people at Paterson. In a conversation with his mother, Aurora, who is explaining that Arturo wants Marcelo to get away from the students at Paterson and to be with "regular people," Marcelo replies, "The children who ride the ponies at Paterson are regular people" (27). Marcelo also wishes to stay at Paterson because "I can learn better there where there is no concern about how Marcelo is different" (33).

The book's critique of "normal" society is strong. When Marcelo's mother talks about her work with children who have cancer, she says, "Sometimes I have to protect them from the so-called 'healthy'" (33). The criticism of society and of how Marcelo is labelled is also clear in a conversation he has with Jasmine when he first meets her. She comes right out and asks him "what's wrong" with him, adding that Arturo had described Marcelo as having a "cognitive disorder," a label that surprises Marcelo. In the conversation that follows, they both question society and its definitions. Marcelo speaks first, then Jasmine:

> "'Cognitive disorder' is not an accurate description of what happens inside Marcelo's head. 'Excessive attempt at cognitive order' is closer to what actually takes place."

> "Yeah? I like excessive order myself. Is that an illness?"

> "If it keeps you from functioning in society the way people think a normal person should, then our society calls that an illness."

> "Well, society is not always right, is it?" (55)

Later on in the conversation he tells Jasmine that his characteristics have some overlap with Asperger's syndrome, but he does not think that label is helpful: "I view myself as different in the way I think, talk, and act, but not as someone who is abnormal or ill" (55).

Other sections also question society's definitions and categories. In discussing with counselor Rabbi Heschel his "special interest" in what he calls "remembering," or thinking deeply about, the Bible, Marcelo points out that he had a friend at Paterson who had special interest in "remembering" baseball. The Rabbi argues that the reason for studying these texts is quite different, and it's not the same thing. Marcelo, however, says, "There is no difference" (273). The point here is that what is considered odd or "not normal" is what society judges to be that way. Although Marcelo is made to believe he is abnormally "obsessed" with religion and sacred texts, plenty of people in the "real" world are obsessed with sports texts and statistics, but that is not deemed abnormal. Throughout the novel, there are repeated questionings of terms and definitions. At the law firm, Marcelo is expected to show progress, but it is "progress as defined by Arturo" (85). Marcelo at first wants to be friends with Wendell, a character whom readers will immediately see as creepy. In his narration, Marcelo wonders "whether anyone considered normal" (87) will be his friend, a speculation readers will find highly ironic, even if Marcelo does not yet fully see Wendell's faults.

In fact, sometimes Marcelo seems almost too angelic, more moral or better than people not diagnosed with what he calls "my condition, whatever that is" (158). His doctor tells him, "In some respects you're about fifty years ahead of other kids your age" (9). When Marcelo is speaking with Rabbi Heschel and says that he "can't imagine how sex can be used for evil," the Rabbi calls him "special" in a way she means to be a compliment. She says, "That's because you are special. You walk with God in Eden" (119). Later in the conversation she says, "It saddens me to know that you will find out soon enough the different ways that we have devised to hurt each other" (120). And when Marcelo decides to turn over the evidence his father's law firm has withheld, he does so not because he wants revenge against his father for having made a pass at Jasmine (266), but out of a moral obligation to do the right thing (266). This super positive portrayal of Marcelo points to another dilemma faced by writers who may be trying to disrupt conventional binaries of abled/disabled. In an attempt perhaps to expose the prejudices about disability—or anything—in the "real" world, writers may end up representing characters like Marcelo as "other" anyway, even if that otherness is "better."

In these two mysteries, *Marcelo in the Real World* and *The London Eye Mystery*, the familiar is made strange as we see it through Marcelo's and Ted's eyes. Because readers see the world through their perspective, it is not their behavior or thinking that seems strange or odd, but that of people in the so-called "normal" world. Both Ted and Marcelo are likable, relatable, and human. Although at times Marcelo seems almost too good, the book succeeds in raising serious questions about society's categories regarding who is "healthy" and who has an "illness" as well as society's treatment of other groups such as women (as sex objects) and Mexican Americans, who faced a very hostile environment at Harvard when Marcelo's father attended. *Marcelo* has a much more serious tone than does *London Eye*, and there are a number of long philosophical discussions about right and wrong. *London Eye* has a much faster pace and it has more humor, though the humor in *Marcelo* is more biting and ironic, perhaps because it is aimed at older teens.

Although both novels do focus on their respective narrator's unusual talent or special interest as the factor that solves the mystery, flirting with making their narrators "supercrips," each text's overall effect disrupts business-as-usual categories and assumptions in society. Both texts raise serious questions about how "normal" is defined, and both are highly critical of society and its contribution to the difficulties each character faces.

From Charlie's Point of View

The title character in Richard Scrimger's 2005 YA mystery novel, *From Charlie's Point of View*, is blind. Charlie's father has been falsely accused of robbing banks, and Charlie and his friends set out to find the real culprit. The story is told in a third person, almost totally omniscient voice, through which we are told the thoughts of not only Charlie, but also his good friend Bernadette, who helps him navigate the world and carry some of his heavy braille equipment. We get an equal peek into the mind of Lewis, their new friend. We even learn the bandit's thoughts, though we don't learn his name until the end. There's an unusual character named Gideon, who is described on the back cover of the book as Charlie's "guardian angel." In the book, Gideon appears almost mysteriously when the children are in trouble, either as a kid on a bike or, later, as a police officer from another district. There is always choir music playing when he arrives on the scene. We are not privy to his thoughts. Although Gideon is more of a force than a main character, it is he who "saves the day" more so than Charlie. He could be a "deus ex machina" device, except that he appears, inexplicably, throughout the novel.

The book begins with the perspective of Bernadette, Charlie's 14-year-old friend. We learn from her that it's the first day of a new school year, when she and her friend Charlie will be starting middle school. The first thing we learn about Charlie, other than that he's been friends with her since kindergarten, is that "he'd be lost without her" (4). In this first scene, we meet Bernadette's chain-smoking, pill-popping mother, who, for breakfast, gives her stale cereal with bugs in it and thinks her daughter is still thirteen. We also learn that although her parents are separated, they are not divorced, and that Bernadette thinks every day about her father coming back. This situation is also important to the plot because it is Bernadette who must come to a realization about her father. She, not Charlie, will be the character who changes the most.

We don't meet Charlie until Scene 2, where we're told about the smells, sounds, and tactile sensations he experiences. We don't know for sure that Charlie is blind until page 14. We're told about his blindness this way: "Charlie's point of view depends mostly on hearing, touch, smell, and imagination. What he actually sees of the world is:" (11). When we turn the page, there are two blank, dark grey pages. We turn the page again, where we're told, "Charlie is blind. Stone blind, bottom-of-a-midnight-well blind. He has been from birth. It doesn't really bother him" (14). These two completely blank, dark grey pages appear four times throughout the novel, first to tell us and then to remind us what it is that Charlie can see: nothing. It's hard to say what effect these pages are supposed to have. Given the silly tone throughout much of the book, the pages are not frightening or even shocking, just unusual. It's doubtful that they're supposed to provide a realistic sense of what blind people perceive. (The author, Richard Scrimger, is described on the back cover as "very nearsighted.")

Charlie's parents are nice enough people, but his father is a cologne-spilling disaster who can't find his socks. At breakfast, they act like teenagers in love, kissing "noisily," much to the amused dismay of Charlie, who says, "You know, there are times when I'm really glad I'm blind" (16). In this scene, we learn that Charlie uses a white cane, and that he has a braille computer called a "Louis Light 200," though Charlie's father can't think of the name of it. The wry tone and humor in this novel is probably meant to appeal to young teens and to suggest that Charlie is just another middle school student with eye-roll inducing parents. His blindness, we're to understand, is simply a fact of his life that he and most people close to him are used to. Ignorant responses to him are mostly limited to new acquaintances or casual encounters with people he meets in school or on the street.

From a disability perspective this is an odd book. Although Bernadette thinks Charlie is "special because he really does seem to be in touch with something that she can't always recognize" (31), he is certainly is not a super hero. Charlie thinks the bandit is Mr. Underglow (214), his educational assistant, but that theory turns out to be wrong. Because of the narrative framework, it's hard to pin down one protagonist. Despite the eponymous title, Charlie is barely the main character. We're not really invited to identify with him, and we actually know very little about him other than being told he is "tall and handsome" (227) and "a natural leader" (219). He participates in the children's investigation, leading the way at one point, walking right into traffic in his pursuit of the bully, Frank, whom he tells to "leave us alone!" (197–201). But even that confrontation is diminished by the twist that Frank has probably been lectured to earlier by Gideon. This scene also shows Charlie walking right out into traffic, waving his cane around, and thinking he's yelling at Frank, but actually "talking to the fire hydrant" (199). So readers are not being asked to identify with Charlie; in this scene, we're being invited to laugh at him.

There also seems to be a mixed message about the level of Charlie's agency. We're shown some equipment that Charlie has and how his educational assistant translates the teacher's notes into braille so that Charlie can do his homework (117). Charlie uses a braille word processor and calculator "about the same size as a hardcover book or a box of chocolates..." (51). His "fingertips touch lightly on the six keys of his Louis Light 200. One key for each of the six spaces in a braille cell" (53). These descriptions may demystify for some readers how some blind students take notes: "Charlie taps along with the teacher, checking what he has written as he goes. The front of the Louis Light 200 displays a running line of braille characters, which he can read and edit" (114). We're also told about the synthesized speech screen-reading program Charlie uses to navigate the web (168), and about a "special ball" he has that makes a sound in the air (182). He plays Monopoly with his friends by feeling the spaces with his fingers and by reading the braille on the game board (225).

However, there are places where Charlie is depicted as being quite dependent on people. We're told that Bernadette "leads Charlie into school" (44) and that "Charlie hangs on Bernadette's elbow" (75). When Charlie's family is considering moving to Winnipeg, Bernadette asks him "What's going to happen to you without me?"—though she also asks what will happen to her without her friend (111). We know that Charlie thinks of himself as "so dependent on others" (113), and we're told that one of Bernadette's worries is "looking after Charlie at school" (123). This dependence is not necessarily depicted as a bad thing. In fact, there's a statement about how we are all dependent on others. When Charlie's friend Bernadette asks him if the "depending on people" that he has to do (25) bothers him, he replies that "everyone depends on someone" (25) and proceeds to give examples, beginning with the bus driver, Alf:

> We're depending on Alf right now to get us to school. He's depending on the people who fill the bus with gas and put up the road signs and traffic lights. They're depending on the people who write the traffic-flow programs for the computers. And *they're* depending on the people who make the microchips. And they are *all* depending on schools to turn out students who know what they're doing. Which is us. (25–26).

This explanation is an insightful example of Eva Kittay's concept of "interdependence" (xii) as an answer to the dependent/independent binary.

We also get some critique of people's ignorance about blindness and treatment of people with disabilities. For example, when riding the elevator in their building, Charlie and Bernadette encounter two people who always ask Charlie what time it is, apparently getting a kick out of the idea that this blind boy always knows the time. These annoying people are, in what will be a disturbing misogynist pattern in this novel and others, "two ladies." One of them, "the older one," is described as "a white-haired knitter." The other one "is a blowsy brunette with a two-packs-a-day-voice" (19). Every time they see Charlie they ask him the time. Bernadette thinks, "How can Charlie put up with people treating him like a freak?" (20). And then one of the "ladies" says, about Charlie: "And so handsome. You'd never suspect anything was wrong with him. If it weren't for the white cane and the sunglasses, you'd swear he was just like anyone else" (21). Readers are supposed to get the irony of this ableist statement because "we" know that Charlie *is* like everyone else.

On the first day of school, when Charlie is saying the Pledge of Allegiance, the narration puts us inside his head, where Charlie is thinking of everyone else in schools across the country who are also saying the pledge: "At this moment he is just like them" (53). Immediately following Charlie's thought, however, the principal, another woman, makes an announcement to the whole school. She refers to Charlie as a "special student" who is—and here she can't bring herself to say "blind"—so she calls him "visually impaired"

(54). She continues to talk about Charlie in the morning announcement, drawing more attention to him in language that belies her plea:

> I want you all to treat him as you would treat a normal--I mean, any other student. Good luck, Charlie. That's all for now, students. My name is Mrs. Vox, and most of you will be seeing me around the school. You'll be hearing me around, Charlie. (54)

This well-intentioned but oblivious principal goes to great lengths to assure us that Charlie is "normal," but her explanation has the opposite effect. This scene, therefore, is meant to skewer politically correct do-gooders who manage to do more harm than good by making a big deal out of something that should go without saying. Another adult, Charlie's educational assistant Mr. Underglow, is patronizing to Charlie. He assumes Charlie either rides a "special bus" or his parents pick him up after school. Charlie informs him that he takes a city bus (118).

In some ways, therefore, this book is a critique of people in society who make negative assumptions about children with disabilities. However, the novel makes this point by drawing on negative assumptions about women. Except for the male bully, Frank, many of the most really obnoxious characters are women, and not young. This disturbing aspect of the book relies on misogynist clichés for humor and for character descriptions. "Little old ladies" are a particularly easy target, as we saw to a lesser extent in *Stoner and Spaz* (Chapter Four). Significantly, as we also saw in Chapter Four, both *True Diary* and *Peeling the Onion* actively and refreshingly work against this stereotype of older women.

In this novel, Frank the bully is on-the-nose evil. He laughs at Charlie because of his blindness and tries to take his sunglasses (47–49). Even Lewis, whom we're supposed to like because he becomes a loyal friend of Charlie and Bernadette, has a telling first reaction when he first meets Charlie. At first, before he notices Charlie is blind, Lewis yammers on and on to both Charlie and Bernadette. In the middle of his yammering, he suddenly stops, notices Charlie is blind, and says, "—hey, you're blind!" (41). Then he immediately starts talking about Charlie to Bernadette:

> He stares at Charlie. Waves his hand in front of Charlie's face. Turns to Bernadette. "He's blind, isn't he? Isn't he?"
>
> There's a pause. "Why don't you ask him?" says Bernadette. (41)

In another section, there's a scene that illustrates society's misunderstanding of disability as well as Charlie's "normality." At lunch one day at school, one child comes over to Charlie and asks him if he can eat a cookie. Charlie asks him why he wouldn't be able to, and then goes on: "I'm blind, that's all. I can eat oatmeal cookies.... I'm really a lot like you" (182).

Some of the name calling in the book is troublesome. A portion of it, of course, is meant to be, because the names certain children call each other is meant to reveal their character flaws. Lewis's mother, who is depicted as a terrible parent, refers to Lewis in public as "my idiot son" (112). That is part of her characterization. But some of the terms seem to be used uncritically, or are used by the omniscient narrator, where the language is not a part of the characterization. Later, Lewis's mother is described by the narrator as "a stout, corseted Gorgon," and Bernadette describes her to Charlie as a "crazy old lady" (176). There are other misogynist and ageist references to older women. It's clear we're not supposed to like Lewis's mother, but even a minor character, the attorney, Madeline Maynard, is described as wearing "stiletto heels, a tiny black dress, and sparkle blue eye shadow, chewing bubble gum" (223). One of the children's classmates, Rachel, is described by the omniscient narrator as "the bimbo" (122). We're told that a woman's house "smells of dust, dog, and old lady" (143). While some of these descriptions are part of characterization, others are not. In her thoughts, Bernadette uses the word "midget" in an analogy, and there is no apparent critique of its use (64). If I were to use this book in a class or discussion group, I'd want to raise some questions about these terms. To read over them without comment simply reinforces the stereotype.

So what is Charlie's role in solving the mystery? It's mixed, which may be a good thing. In spite of the title, the book is not really from Charlie's point of view. We get inside his head occasionally, as we do many of the other characters, and there is one chapter entitled "Charlie's POV" which is when he volunteers to crawl through the dark, narrow tunnel in the graveyard, near the climax of the book. He does lead the way occasionally (197) and he stands up to Frank, the bully (199).

But Charlie is not the central character. Not only does the book begin with Bernadette's point of view, the last scene is also hers. At the end, she is able to recognize that her father is an alcoholic who will probably never change. Charlie is a likable character but remains the same throughout: tall, handsome, steady, and dependable. Charlie has the main conflict of the book—his father being falsely accused of robbing banks—but he has no inner conflicts or troublesome family members to deal with. He doesn't need to grow or change, and he doesn't. About halfway through the novel, however, Bernadette has an inner thought to which we are privy. She resolves to one day "do something just for me" (154). In the last paragraph of the book she wears makeup, and the last line of the book is, "This is for her" (278).

Like many YA novels, this one depicts many of the parents as either incompetent and foolish or downright malevolent. Charlie's father is nice enough, though a bit spacy. His mother can't seem to put her arm in the right position to guide Charlie in a helpful way, or to give him proper directions for getting onto an escalator (205). Bernadette's mother is always drunk, and her daughter has to literally step over her. She spouts ignorant sayings and generally makes Bernadette's life miserable, and she's the parent who did not abandon the family. Lewis's parents fight constantly, and one is cheating on the other. The best parents in this book manage to not be intoxicated, absent, or mean, but they are usually over-protective and oblivious. Like many mystery novels, there are a number of suspicious characters and red herrings, and although the accusation against Charlie's father is serious, the omniscient narrator seems to have a humorous approach to the events, so it's hard to take any of this seriously.

This novel would educate some readers regarding the equipment Charlie uses, such as his braille word processor/calculator. We're told about his braille notes being translated (160) so he can work on disk. There's a lot of emphasis on the fact that Charlie is very attuned to smell, hearing, and to tactile senses. It does, therefore, suggest a view of the world "from Charlie's point of view." It shows some perspective about other senses and how Charlie can function in the darkness when others cannot. He uses those other senses as he crawls through the graveyard tunnel and tries to find a way out. He's brave, and he can navigate in the dark, which the others cannot do. At one point, he says he feels sorry for sighted people because they must be afraid in the dark, which he is not. (In that way he is like Rudolph on the foggy Christmas Eve, in that he can maneuver in the dark when the sighted, "normal" children cannot.) Although the three children do solve the mystery and Charlie's talents play a part, it is Gideon, the mysterious guardian angel figure, who actually saves the day throughout the novel, and Bernadette is the only character who shows any growth.

The text is somewhat successful depicting Charlie as a "normal" boy, even if some of the unlikable characters don't see him that way. He goes to class, does his homework, rides the bus with his friends, plays Monopoly, and enjoys TV. This book, therefore, is an interesting cultural artifact useful mostly for what cultural assumptions it questions (that blind children can't do homework or enjoy TV shows) and what cultural assumptions it exploits. In some scenes, however, Charlie looks very dependent on Bernadette and the absurd walking-in-traffic scene does not add to his dignity.

While there is some positive cultural work accomplished by *From Charlie's Point of View* and some challenging of assumptions regarding people who are blind, this positive work comes at the expense of some powerful cementing of ageist and gender stereotypes. The book exposes the prejudiced and ignorant society Charlie lives in, though it is too often stereotypical "little old ladies" who are this way. Therefore, many of the possibilities for critiquing society are dissipated by simply having a ready-made scapegoat: older women. And in spite of having his name in the title, Charlie is a rather one-dimensional character. Other than the likable, smart, and loyal Bernadette, who is really more of a protagonist than Charlie, almost all the other women or girls, even minor characters, are clichés that tap into ugly stereotypes.

Young contributors on Goodreads seem to enjoy the book, and virtually all the reviewers mention Charlie's blindness and how intrigued and surprised they are that he can solve a mystery. If this book is used in a classroom, however, students may need some guidance to be critical readers. In her section of a longer article in *Disability Studies Quarterly*, Lisa Patterson poses a useful question about *From Charlie's Point of View*: "Scrimger includes scenes throughout the book in which Charlie is compared to (or in some cases, contrasted with) 'everyone else.' How does this position readers to think about blindness and disability?" (Walker, Mileski, Greaves, and Patterson). Here are other questions that might enrich a class discussion of *From Charlie's Point of View*. They may be modified, of course, to better fit an analysis of other texts:

- What conventions of a mystery story does this novel follow? Which ones does it break?
- What do you think about the narrative point of view in this novel?
- To what extent is Charlie a fully developed character?
- What do you think of the way the parents are portrayed in the book? Why do you think they are portrayed in that way?
- What did you think about blindness before you read this book?
- Did this book make you think any differently about blindness?
- How does Charlie depend on Bernadette? How does she depend on him?

- How do some people react to Charlie, once they realize he's blind? Find some examples of how they treat him differently or what assumptions they make about him. What do you think of this treatment or these assumptions?
- How are some women characterized in this book, especially older women? Find some examples. How many of the "bad" or obnoxious characters are men? Compare the descriptions of these characters. What do you think about these characterizations?
- Who is narrating this story? What do you think of this narrator? What makes you think that?

While this YA mystery is useful for its semi-focus on a blind detective, it also has the potential for doing some cultural damage if not discussed with readers. Teachers posing high-level, open questions can help challenge stereotypes, disability myths, and harmful cultural assumptions.

The Dark Days of Hamburger Halpin

Josh Berk's 2010 YA novel, *The Dark Days of Hamburger Halpin*, was discussed in Chapter Two for its relevance to respect and etiquette. It is also relevant in this chapter on talents, Rudolph stories, and "supercrips." The sixteen-year-old narrator, Will Halpin, has just transferred from Paterson, a school for the deaf, to the public Carbon High School because he thought his classmates at Paterson were too political and too critical of the hearing world, a view Will rejected in the past but now reconsiders given his treatment at Carbon High (8). Will, whose texting name is Hamburger Halpin, is a long way from being a superhero. We find out in the second sentence that he wears "plus size" clothes. He also makes frequent self-deprecating comments about his weight and he is always telling us how much he eats. He can speak but hardly ever does because people "have laughed at the way I talk" (6). Two big advantages to finding clues to the mystery come through Will's highly developed ability at sign language and lipreading. As is hinted at and then confirmed during the big reveal at the end, Will also has a talent (bordering on a superpower) for vision.

Like Rudolph, Will has no friends at the start of the story and his classmates either ignore him or call him names. By the end, he solves the mystery and he has a good friend and the potential for a girlfriend. He doesn't do it alone, however. Like many classic sleuths, he has a sidekick and helper, in this case a fellow outcast and future friend Devon Smiley, who initiates some of the sleuthing and figures out the bully Pat Chambers' password. Will and Devon are also helped by Will's ex-girlfriend Ebony from his old school, who helps with the lipreading needed to solve the crime. This novel is much lighter in tone than is *Marcelo*, although some of the events could have warranted more serious treatment (a student pushed to his death, a teacher sleeping with her underage student, a young woman impregnated through a possible rape by a bully).

During a class trip to an old coal mine, when the lights are cut off for a minute so that students can experience the dramatic effect of total darkness underground, the bully disappears. His body is soon found at the bottom of a ledge, and it's determined that he was pushed. The mystery is figuring out who pushed him. Since the victim bullied almost everyone, there are many possible suspects, including the narrator. To add to the drama, this coal mine is reputedly haunted by a deaf miner who supposedly became trapped and died there over 100 years ago. He had Will's same name, William Halpin, though he was called "Dummy" Halpin by his co-workers in that era, a fact that makes Will ashamed.

This novel also flirts with being a Rudolph story because of Will's extra-keen vision and his "fantastic" (2) lipreading skills. Sometimes the character uses realistic aptitudes for observation, as many mystery novel protagonists do, to figure out who did it. But sometimes Will taps into unusual skills, developed because of his deafness, to see things others have missed. It's left open as to whether these skills are natural or, like Rudolph's glowing nose, a bit beyond that. Will refers to "the sort of sneak deaf detection I'm aces at" (10) and says that he has "a good sense of smell" (12). He says that "deaf people definitely sense things" (71) and that deaf people "are also good at reading emotion as well as content" (8–9). He also says, "There are ways that what makes you different makes you stronger" (47). These qualities, especially the keen sight that plays the biggest part of solving the mystery, are very close to the "compensations" typical in "supercrip" stories described above. Whether Will's keen sense of seeing or observing is a special gift or compensation is left ambiguous. While there is a suggestion that Will has an almost supernatural vision, the text leaves room for this vision to be simply an alertness that anyone could have. In each case, as soon as Will suggests that he has a special talent, he undermines that suggestion with a question.

Early in the novel, he sees something in beautiful classmate Leigha's eyes that tells him something is bothering her: "There is a melancholy around her eyes that the world misses, that no one else can see. Except me?" (80). We find out much later, through lipreading, that Leigha is pregnant by the bully, who either raped or coerced her. In some online photos that the bully has posted of Leigha in a "mostly unclothed" (159) position on the bully's bed, Will sees that "Her eyes are vacant, and her mouth is tight and grim, like she's scared. Was she? Devon pats me on the back in a consoling way. Thanks? Does he notice what I see in her face? Is it really there, or am I just wishing?" (160).

It is again Will's astute vision that helps him make out the outline of a door in the mine that none of the investigators noticed. In his narration, Will raises the possibility of having a special "instinct," and then simultaneously makes fun of this possibility, telling us there was a note carved into the cave:

> A secret passage! And something tells me, an instinct, that many years ago my ances-tor, the original Will Halpin, had been in this exact spot.
>
> Or maybe, just maybe, it is these words, clawed into the rock: DUMMY WAS HERE. (202).

This door leads to a secret passageway that his namesake from the last century, "Dummy" Halpin, took to escape the mine disaster, and it was also the way the murderer took on the day the bully Pat Chambers was pushed to his death.

Although he has help from friends Devon and Ebony, it is also Will's vision again that ultimately solves the mystery. Will actually sees the one who pushed the bully begin to move toward him during the brief period of darkness in the mine. When they turned the lights out in the mine tour, Devon took a photo of the dark. In that bright flash Will tells us, "I saw someone. At the edge of the mine. Next to Pat. Emerging from the wall" (235). Although it is early in the novel that he sees this character—who turns out to be Leigha—in the flash of the camera, this fact is not revealed until the last chapter, right before the Epilogue. Will is immediately famous in the local community, get-ting "top billing" in the local media and, "My name was even briefly on CNN. com as the "Pennsylvania deaf high school student" who solves the mystery (240). This scene parallels all the reindeers loving Rudolph at the end of that song. But when read with the other, more ambiguous scenes involving Will's talent, there is still some room for his powers of observation to be simply the result of his interest in Leigha and in the deaf miner who had his same name.

If teachers or discussion leaders assign this novel, a good question for read-ers might be, "To what extent do you think Will's talents (excellent lipreading and signing skills, extra keen vision and observation skills) are the result of his deafness?" It would also be helpful for students to read (or otherwise learn about) the "overcoming or compensation" disability myth discussed earlier, with a follow up question: "How might fictional characters with disabilities being given a special 'gift' or 'compensation' actually be harmful to real people with impairments?"

Like the other novels discussed in this chapter, this one also critiques society's treatment of people who are deaf or hard of hearing. It's a much gentler critique than are *Accidents of Nature* and *Peeling the Onion* (discussed in previous chapters), both of which were written by authors with a disability similar to that of the respective narrators. According to information in the Acknowledgments pages in *Dark Days*, the author researched deaf issues by reading "deaf writers and bloggers who helped me understand my subject better without even knowing it" (250). The back inside flap says that he also researched "the condition by getting to know folks who are and by 'lurking' on deaf blogs and message boards, reading books, and consulting with a deaf librarian and a fellow author." The term "hearing-impaired" is also used in that description. It's unfortunate that these biographical materials do not use the preferred term, "hard-of-hearing."

This novel has some positive qualities. Readers who haven't thought about such things before would learn from Will about television having "weird [closed] captioning goof-ups" (121). As discussed in Chapter Two, Will's new public school is ill equipped to provide resources like captioning or interpreters. Many teachers and students have no idea how to make his experience there more inclusive, and Will comments on "how little people around here seem to know about being deaf" (100). Rude or oblivious characters cover their mouths or turn away from Will, even though they know he needs to lipread. A substitute teacher merely shouts at him. Will sometimes points out language that privileges a hearing world. He objects to what he calls an "offensive term" (46) like "ticked," which is related to sound. He also insists on the computer term "selected" instead of "clicked on" for the same reason (77, 80), though he has no problem using "lame" as an adjective uncritically (82).

This novel is refreshing in its highlighting of many creative ways to communicate that do not involve speech. Sign language comes across as being both difficult to learn and very cool. Characters sign ridiculous things to non-signers as mini-protests, so the non-signers are seen as dolts and the few people who do know sign are able to have a hidden conversation from those who don't. Devon can finger spell and he learns some sign language phrases throughout the story. Sometimes Will and Devon simply write notes back and forth, but they also each have a handheld personal device called a Crony which enables them to instant message and text (130). When there is no reception down in the mine they use white boards with dry-erase markers. One time Will breathes on a car window and writes in the steam and another time he writes a note in the dirt. Although Will's first person narrator tells most of the story, we also obtain lots of information through these alternate modes, which makes some of these tools or languages less exotic to those unfamiliar with them and breaks up the narrative in interesting ways.

Will's ex-girlfriend Ebony from Paterson is also a great lipreader. He describes her political views, some of which Will does not totally embrace. He says, for example, that "I simply don't have a problem with hearing people" (8), though after a half day at Carbon High, "now I'm not so sure...." (8). He says Ebony "gets really mad about the idea that deafness is a disability and something you need to be cured of" (172). By having this view expressed by Ebony and not the first-person narrator they may be identifying with, readers new to what they may see as more radical concepts in Deaf culture may be better able to absorb them because they are related by Will, who is not at either end of that controversy, but more in the middle.

As is almost a tradition in YA novels, the narrator has some unflattering descriptions of many adults he encounters, as might be expected from a bullied sixteen-year old. The most vicious descriptions, however, (as in *From Charlie's Point of View*) are reserved for girls and women, especially older women. Some of the men have vivid and negative descriptions too, of course, but the descriptions of even minor female characters seem personal. Only three paragraphs into the novel, the school superintendent is described as "a woman who looks like a skeleton in a Beatles wig and smells like beef" (2). A minor character, a substitute teacher, is described this way: "A wildebeest in a lime green pants suit. Lipstick smeared on thicker than tar on a country road, and enough rouge to choke a horse" (229). Even Will's mother, who we think may finally be a not-so-bad parent because she has learned sign language and "never makes me read her lips, even though it would be easier for her" (42), has bullying qualities. In criticizing his father, Will says, "Why does he let Mom bully him? Bully both of us?" (47).

As of this writing there are not a lot of reviews or discussion questions regarding *Dark Days*. The website CommonSensemedia.org mostly just reports on the mention of drugs and sexual references in the novel. One notable review is from "Ana" at The Book Smugglers website in which the writer contrasts the US and UK covers, the former being cartoonish and juvenile, the latter shadowy and serious. As The Book Smugglers writer cogently argues, these two covers may suggest a difficulty the publishers had in trying to characterize this book. Is it mostly a light, humorous mystery, or does it raise important social issues? A book can do both, of course, as the review also suggests, but there are enough serious issues raised in this book that go unaddressed: homophobia (pointed out in The Book Smugglers review) misogyny, pedophilia, a possible rape, and, of course, the possibility of an almost supernatural talent held by the deaf narrator. These issues are not treated seriously at all, and, in fact, may be playing to unexamined assumptions in society. While *Dark Days* has potential to open up productive conversations about disability, sexism, and other prejudices in society, teachers or discussion leaders would be advised to have some questions to pose about this text similar to the ones posed above regarding *From Charlie's Point of View*. Students might discuss the open issue regarding Will's acute vision, and whether this talent is a "compensatory ability" Dolmage foregrounds as being problematic. A class discussion could also include the barriers Will faces when he leaves the deaf school, as well as the bullying or ignorant behavior of some of the people he encounters. I'd also want to examine with students some of the serious issues the novel skirts, as well as some of the characterizations, especially of women.

I look forward to the book eventually being reviewed on the Disability in Kidlit website. This site, focused on disability-themed YA literature, solicits reviews of these texts "done by people who share the disability under discussion—or at least a similar one" (Disability in Kidlit website). As of this writing, there was no review there yet for *Dark Days*, though the site had the book listed as up for review.

So Are They 'Rudolph' Stories?

Disability-themed mystery novels with "disabled" sleuths can reveal to some readers the contributions people with impairments can make to society, using talents or insights they have developed, sometimes because of their specific impairment. Such texts can also make the category called "normal" more expansive or call the whole concept of normality into question.

For some readers, thinking about contributions such characters make to society may be the first time they have considered this idea. In such cases, the novel may function in a way similar to the "awakening" stories (Royster) or "enlightenment narratives" (Vidali, Price, Lewiecki-Wilson) discussed in

Chapter Three. Such stories can provide one perspective on disability that some non-disabled readers have not thought about before. Though these stories are not necessary for those who have experienced racism in our society or, by extension, for those who have experienced ableism, these stories can help some non-disabled readers better understand the barriers people with disability face in our society. As mentioned earlier, however, as Vidali, Price, and Lewiecki-Wilson point out regarding "enlightenment narratives," such tales run the risk of inviting non-disabled readers to think that people with disabilities are there to somehow teach non-disabled people something.

In all four of the mysteries analyzed in this chapter these issues are worth discussing with students. In all four cases it is noteworthy that the character does not solve the crime by himself. This group effort occurs in *From Charlie's Point of View*, where Charlie is helped by Bernadette, Lewis, and the handy guardian angel Gideon. Ted and his sister eventually work together in *The London Eye Mystery*, each using what they're good at to "sort it out." Marcelo gets good advice from his rabbi, as well as a lot of help from co-worker Jasmine, who actually locates the important file needed by Ixtel, the injured girl Marcelo is trying to help. Will's friend Devon in *Dark Days* provides some key information as does his lipreading friend, Ebony. Ultimately, however, it is the main character's impairment that plays a big role in the story. Charlie, who is blind, makes his way through the dark when others cannot. Ted's extreme logic from his "syndrome" helps him eliminate false theories. Marcelo's "special interest" in religion and morality help him decide to help Ixtel. Will's lipreading and well-developed sense of sight help him see things others do not.

Whether the impairment in each case becomes like Rudolph's red nose, a "compensation" or a "gift" of the type that fits the stereotype Dolmage describes above, the kind that can simply substitute one form of abnormality for another, is not completely resolved. Some of these novels question some myths but reinscribe others. Some are better written than others. Some are more critical than others of the society that plays a role in disabling the main character. *Marcelo* and *London Eye* are much more complex and nuanced than the others in their representation of their narrators, and these two novels are also much more critical of the role society plays in misunderstanding the character with the impairment or in partly causing the disability. *London Eye* accomplishes this with a much lighter touch than does *Marcelo*, but *Marcelo* is also written for older teens.

All four novels warrant discussion. As with many other texts that young people read, these texts need to have questions posed about them designed to help students see, name, and confront harmful assumptions, whether about race, religion, sexual orientation, age, gender, or disability and whether those assumptions come from clueless characters or from "neutral" omniscient narrators. It is in grappling with such questions about representation in fiction that readers can extend their analysis into representations of disability in other texts and in the world they live in.

Note

1. Following British conventions, *London Eye* uses single quotations around dialogue. For the sake of consistency, however, I will put dialogue in double quotations.

WORKS CITED

Alexie, Sherman. *The Absolutely True Diary of a Part-Time Indian*. New York: Little, Brown and Company, 2007.

Ana. "Book Review: *The Dark Days of Hamburger Halpin* by Josh Berk." The Book Smugglers. March 29, 2011.Web. 23 June 2014.

Andrews, Sharon E. "Using Inclusion Literature to Promote Positive Attitudes Toward Disabilities." *Journal of Adolescent and Adult Literacy* 41.6 (March 1998): 420–426.

Arastu, Aleema. "Aleema Arastu's Review." Rev. of *Peeling the Onion*, by Wendy Orr. *Goodreads*. 5 May 2013. Web. 6 Feb. 2014.

Arndt, Katrina, Julia M. White, and Andrea Chervenak. "'Gotta Go Now': Rethinking the Use of *The Mighty* and *Simon Birch* In the Middle School Classroom." *Disability Studies Quarterly* 30.1 (2010).

Baskin, Barbara Holland and Karen H. Harris. *More Notes from a Different Drummer: A Guide to Juvenile Fiction Portraying the Disabled*. New York: R. R. Bowker Company, 1984.

Beam, Diana. "*The Acorn People* Reading Guide and Notes." n.d. Augusta Country Public Schools, Verona, VA. N.d. Web. 24 June 2012.

Berman, Matt. Rev. of *Stoner and Spaz*, by Ron Koertge. *Common Sense Media*. 24 April 2004. Web. 5 Feb. 2014.

Bérubé, Michael. "Disability and Narrative." *PMLA* 120.2 (March 2005): 568–576.

_____. *Life As We Know It: A Father, a Family, and an Exceptional Child*. Random House, 1996. Print.

Berk, Josh. *The Dark Days of Hamburger Halpin*. New York: Alfred A. Knopf, 2010.

Bernstein, Adam. "Theodore Taylor, 85; Author of 'The Cay' [Obituary]/ *Washington Post*. 30 October 2006. Web. 6 July 2014.

Biklen, Douglas, Robert Bogdan, and Burton Blatt. "Label Jars, Not People." In *Promise and Performance: Children with Special Needs: ACT's Guide to TV Programming for Children*. Ed. Maureen Harmonay. Cambridge, MA: Ballinger, 1977. 3–10.

"BookRags Student Essay." No author. *"Peeling the Onion*, a Review." Rev. of *Peeling the Onion*, by Wendy Orr. *BookRags, Inc*. 23 Oct 2004. Web. 3 March 2014.

Brenna, Bev. "Characters with Disabilities in Contemporary Novels for Children: A Portrait of Three Authors in a Framework of Canadian Texts." *Language and Literacy* 13.1 (Spring 2011): 1–12.

Bruce, Heather E., Anna E. Baldwin, and Christabel, Umphrey. *"Flight* and *The Absolutely True Diary of a Part-Time Indian*: Post-9/11 Hope and Reconciliation." In *Sherman Alexie in the Classroom*. Urbana, IL, NCTE, 2008. 111–131.

Carroll, Pamela S. and L. Penny Rosenblum. "Through Their Eyes: Are Characters with Visual Impairment Portrayed Realistically in Young Adult Literature?" *Journal of Adolescent & Adult Literacy* 43.7 (April 2000): 620–630.

Chapel, Jessica. "American Literature." (Interview with Sherman Alexie). Atlantic Unbound. *The Atlantic Online*. 1 June 2000. Web. 6 Jan 2014.

Charlton, James I. *Nothing About Us Without Us: Disability Oppression and Empowerment*. Berkeley: University of California Press, 2000. Print.

Cline, Lynn. "About Sherman Alexie: A Profile." *Ploughshares* 26.4 (Winter 2000/2001): 197–202.

Crandall, Bryan Ripley. "Adding a Disability Perspective When Reading Adolescent Literature: Sherman Alexie's *The Absolutely True Diary of a Part-Time Indian*." *The ALAN Review* (Winter 2009): 71–78.

Crowley, Sharon and Debra Hawhee. *Ancient Rhetorics for Contemporary Students*.Fourth Edition. New York: Pearson/Longman, 2009.

Cummins, Amy. Rev. of *Accidents of Nature*, by Harriet McBryde Johnson. *Disability Studies Quarterly* 28.2 (Spring 2008) Web. 11 May 2012.

Curwood, Jen Scott. "Redefining Normal: A Critical Analysis of (Dis)ability in Young Adult Literature. *Children's Literature in Education* 44.1 (March 2013): 15–28.

Dolmage, Jay. *Disability Rhetoric*. Syracuse: Syracuse University Press, 2014.

Dowd, Siobhan. *The London Eye Mystery*. New York: Random House, 2007.

Ehrenreich, Barbara. *Bright-Sided: How Positive Thinking is Undermining America*. New York: Picador, 2009.

Fetterley, Judith. *The Resisting Reader: A Feminist Approach to American Fiction*. Bloomington: Indiana University Press, 1978. Print.

Fryer, Jonathan. "Siobhan Dowd: Author and Human Rights Campaigner Who Defended Jailed Writers." Obituary. *The Guardian*. 23 August 2007. Web.

Gabel, Susan Lynn. "Introduction: Disability Studies in Education." In *Disability Studies in Education: Readings and Method*. Susan Lynn Gabel. Ed. New York: Peter Lang Publishing, Inc. 2005, 2009. (1–20).

Haller, Beth. "What was Traditional News Media Advocacy for Disability Advocates? Part 1." N.d. Web. *Disability Advocacy through Media Training Course*. Unit 2. 11 June 2013.

Hazlett, Lisa A., William J. Sweeney, and Kevin J. Reins. "Using Young Adult Literature Featuring LGBTQ Adolescents with Intellectual and/or Physical Disabilities to Strengthen Classroom Inclusion." *Theory Into Practice* 50.3 (2011): 206–214.

Heilker, Paul and Melanie Yergeau. "Autism and Rhetoric." *College English* 73.5 (May 2011): 485–497.

Heiser, Madison. "The Scarlet Ibis Reading Response." "Madisonheiserblogspot." 7 March 2011. Web. 10 May 2014.

Hurst, James. "The Scarlet Ibis." *The Atlantic Monthly*. July 1960. Web. 1 June 2014.

Jenafer. "Jenafer's Reviews." Rev. of *Peeling the Onion*, by Wendy Orr. *GoodReads*. 9 Feb. 2011. Web. 8 Feb. 2014.

John, Antony. *Five Flavors of Dumb*. New York: Dial Books, The Penguin Group, 2010.

Johnson, Harriet McBryde. *Accidents of Nature*. New York: Henry Holt and Company, 2006.

____ *Too Late to Die Young: Nearly True Tales from a Life*. New York: Henry Holt and Company, 2005.

Jones, Ron. *The Acorn People*. New York: Random House, 1976.

Keith, Lois. *Take Up Thy Bed & Walk: Death, Disability and Cure in Classic Fiction for Girls*. New York: Routledge, 2001.

"Kirkus Review." (no author). Rev. of *Peeling the Onion*, by Wendy Orr. *Kirkus Reviews*. 1 Feb 1997. Web. 7 Jan. 2014.

Kittay, Eva Fetter. *Love's Labor: Essays on Women, Equality and Dependency*. New York: Routledge, 1999. Print.

Klipper, Barbara. "Great Reads, Intriguing Characters: The Schneider Family Book Award Winners." *Young Adult Library Services* (Spring 2011): 6–7.

Koertge, Ron. *Stoner and Spaz*. Cambridge, MA: Candlewick Press, 2004.

____. "Good Hands." In *Owning It: Stories about Teens with Disabilities*. Ed. Don R. Gallo. Cambridge, MA: Candlewick Press, 2008. 101–118. Print.

Kurtts, Stephanie A. and Karen Gavigan. "Understanding (Dis)abilities through Children's Literature. *Education Libraries* 31.1 (Summer 2008): 23–31.

Landrum, Judith E. "Adolescent Novels that Feature Characters with Disabilities: An Annotated Bibliography." *Journal of Adolescent & Adult Literacy* 42.4 (December1998/January 1999): 284–290.

Lazarescu, Sara. "Stoner and Spaz." Rev. of *Stoner and Spaz*, by Ron Koertge. *Sara Can Read*. 6 June 2013. Web. 3 January 3, 2014. http://harrypotterismyboyfriend.blogspot.com/2013/06/stoner-spaz.html

Letcher, Mark. "Autism in Young Adult Literature." ("Off the Shelves" column) *English Journal* 100.2 (November 2010): 113–116. Print.

Lewiecki-Wilson, Cynthia, Brenda Jo Brueggemann, with Jay Dolmage (Eds.) *Disability and the Teaching of Writing: A Critical Sourcebook*. Boston and New York: Bedford/St. Martins, 2008. Print.

Lewiecki-Wilson, Cynthia. "Ableist Rhetorics, Nevertheless: Disability and Animal Rights in the Work of Peter Singer and Martha Nussbaum." *JAC: Rhetoric, Writing, Culture, Politics* 31.1–2 (2011): 71–101. Print.

Linton, Simi. *Claiming Disability, Knowledge and Identity*. New York and London: New York University Press. 1998. Print.

Martin, Deb. "Add Disability and Stir: The New Ingredient in Composition Textbooks." In *Disability and the Teaching of Writing: A Critical Sourcebook*. Eds. Cynthia Lewiecki-Wilson, Brenda Jo Brueggemann, with Jay Dolmage. Boston and New York: Bedford/St. Martin's, 2008: 74–91. Print.

McNally, Joel. "Sherman Alexie: Tough, Smart, Funny and Not about to Back Off From His Indian Roots." *The Writer*. 114.6 (June 2011): 28–31.

Meekosha, Helen and Russell Shuttleworth. "What's so 'Critical' about Critical Disability Studies?" *Australian Journal of Human Rights* 15.1 (2009): 47–75.

Menchetti, Bruce, Gina Plattos, and Pamela S. Carroll. "The Impact of Fiction on Perceptions of Disability. *The ALAN Review* (Fall 2011): 56–66.

Merritt, Tonya. "Finding the Will to Individualize Instruction: How My Son Made Me a Better Teacher." *English Journal* 100.2 (Nov 2010): 49–55. Print.

Mitchell, David T. and Sharon L. Snyder. *Narrative Prosthesis: Dependencies on Discourse*. Ann Arbor, MI: University of Michigan Press, 2000. Chapter Two, "Narrative Prosthesis and the Materiality of Metaphor." 47–64.

Newton, Deanne. "Peeling the Onion." Rev. of *Peeling the* Onion, by Wendy Orr. *Divine: A Community for and by People with Disabilities*. 7 October 2012. Web. 3 March 2014.

"Ninth Grade Resources." McDougal Littell Language of Literature. n.d. *CurriculumCompanionlite*. Web. 6 June 2014.

Orr, Wendy. *Peeling the Onion*. New York: Random House, 1996.

Orr, Wendy. "Teachers' Resources: *Peeling the Onion Study Guide."* Wendy Orr Journal. 9 April 2012. Web. 6 Jan. 2014.

Orr, Wendy. "The Unreliable Narrator: Writing in the First Person." *Wendy Orr Journal*. 5 Feb. 2012. Web. 16 May 2014.

"Peeling the Onion." (No author) Review of *Peeling the Onion*, by Wendy Orr. *Publishers Weekly*. 1 April 1997 Web. 5 April 2014.

Poe, Edgar Allan. "The Poetic Principle." *Home Journal* 36 (August 31. 1850): 1+.

Prater, Mary Anne, "Learning Disabilities in Children's and Adolescent Literature: How Are Characters Portrayed?" *Learning Disability Quarterly* 26 (Winter 2003): 47–62.

Rousso, Harilyn. *Don't Call Me Inspirational: A Disabled Feminist Talks Back*. Philadelphia: Temple University Press, 2013.

Rowell, Charles H. "An Interview with Chinua Achebe." *Callaloo* 13.1 (Winter, 1990): 86–101).

Royster, Jacqueline Jones. "Sarah's Story: Making a Place for Historical Ethnography in Rhetorical Studies." In *Rhetoric, the Polis, and the Global Village: Proceedings from the 1998 Rhetoric Society of America Conference*. Eds. C. Jan Swearington and Dave Pruett. Mahwah: Lawrence Erlbaum Associates. 1991. 39–51.

Sachar, Louis. *The Cardturner*. New York: Delacorte, 2010.

Saunders, Kathy. "What Disability Studies Can Do For Children's Literature." *Disability Studies Quarterly* 24.1 (Winter 2004). Web. Retrieved March 1, 2014.

Scales, Pat. "Teachers Guide." *The Cay*. April 2013. *Teachers at Random* [Random House]. Web. 4 July 2014.

Schwartz, Albert V. "THE CAY: Racism Rewarded." *Interracial Books for Children*, 1971.

Scrimger, Richard. *From Charlie's Point of View*. Toronto, Ontario: Tundra Books, 2005.

Selwochi, Barbara and Michelle Dunn. "Mystery and Meaning: A WebQuest for 9th Grade English Journey of the Self." N.d. Anne Arundel County Public Schools. 15 Aug 1999. Web. 6 June 2014.

Shapiro, Joseph. P. *No Pity: People with Disabilities Forging a New Civil Rights Movement*. New York: Random House. 1994.

Sherman, Krista. "Inclusive Stories: Teaching About Disabilities With Picture Books." Unit Plan *Read/Write/Think*. National Council of Teachers of English. n.d. Web. 14 July 2012.

Shmoop Editorial Team. "Intro" [to "The Scarlet Ibis"] 11 Nov. 2008. Web. *Shmoop.com*. Shmoop University Inc. 3 July 2014.

Sieruta, Peter D. "This One Really Did Happen." 7 April 2009. *Collecting Children's Books*. Web. 4 July 2014.

Smith, Robin M. and Nirmala Erevelles. "Towards an Enabling Education: The Difference that Disability Makes." Review of Longmore's Why I Burned My Book and Other Essays on Disability and Michalko's *The Difference That Disability Makes*. *Educational Researcher* 33.8 (November 2004) 31–36.

"Mission & History." *Society for Disability Studies*. N.d. Web. 5 Feb 2013.

Starke, Jacqueline. "The Acorn People: A Webquest for 7th Grade Reading." Webquest. New Franklin R-1 Schools (Missouri). 26 March 2008. Web. 14 July 2012.

Stork, Francisco X. *Marcelo in the Real World*. New York: Scholastic, 2009.

Tal, Eve. "Swimming the Mainstream: A Discussion of Criteria for Evaluating Children's Literature about Disabilities." *Bookbird*. Basel 39.1 (2001): 30–33.

Tawny. "Tawny's Review." Rev. of *Peeling the Onion*, by Wendy Orr. *Goodreads*. 31 May 2010. Web. 5 Feb. 2014.

Taylor, Theodore. *The Cay and Related Readings*. Evanston, IL: McDougal Littell. 1998.

"The Scarlet Ibis." Wikipedia. 24 July 2014. Web. 10 Aug 2014.

"The Scarlet Ibis." Wikispaces.com. n.d. Web. 6 June 2014.

Tompkins, Jane. *Sensational Designs: The Cultural Work of American Fiction 1790–1860*. New York: Oxford University Press. 1985. Print.

Tretler, Marcia. "Novel Ties, *The Cay*, A Study Guide." New York, *Learning Links Inc*. 1986, 2003. Web. 7 July 2014.

Trites, Roberta Seelinger. *Disturbing the Universe: Power and Repression in Adolescent Literature*. Iowa City: University of Iowa Press, 2000.

Vidali, Amy, Margaret Price, and Cynthia Lewiecki-Wilson. "Introduction: Disability Studies in the Undergraduate Classroom." *Disability Studies Quarterly* 28.4 (2008). Web. 13 July 2012.

Walker, Valerie Struthers, Tara Mileski, Dana Greaves, and Lisa Patterson. "Questioning Representations of Disability in Adolescent Literature: Reader Response Meets Disability Studies." *Disability Studies Quarterly* 28.4 (2008). Web. 13 July, 2012.

Wopperer, Emily. "Inclusive Literature in the Library and the Classroom." *Knowledge Quest* 39.3 (January/February 2011): 26–34.

INDEX

Disability Studies in Education

GENERAL EDITORS: SUSAN L. GABEL & SCOT DANFORTH

The book series Disability Studies in Education is dedicated to the publication of monographs and edited volumes that integrate the perspectives, methods, and theories of disability studies with the study of issues and problems of education. The series features books that further define, elaborate upon, and extend knowledge in the field of disability studies in education. Special emphasis is given to work that poses solutions to important problems facing contemporary educational theory, policy, and practice.

To order other books in this series, please contact our Customer Service Department:

> (800) 770-LANG (within the U.S.)
> (212) 647-7706 (outside the U.S.)
> (212) 647-7707 FAX

Or browse by series:

WWW.PETERLANG.COM